Keeping the feast

Metaphors for the Meal

MILTON BRASHER-CUNNINGHAM

Morehouse Publishing

NEW YORK · HARRISBURG · DENVER

Unless otherwise noted, the Scripture quotations contained herein are from the New Revised Standard Version Bible, copyright © 1989 by the Division of Christian Education of the National Council of Churches of Christ in the U.S.A. Used by permission. All rights reserved.

Morehouse Publishing, 4775 Linglestown Road, Harrisburg, PA 17112

Morehouse Publishing, 445 Fifth Avenue, New York, NY 10016

Morehouse Publishing is an imprint of Church Publishing Incorporated.

www.churchpublishing.org

Cover design by Laurie Klein Westhafer
Typeset by Denise Hoff
Back cover photo by Mark Branly

Library of Congress Cataloging-in-Publication Data

Brasher-Cunningham, Milton.
Keeping the feast : metaphors for the meal / Milton Brasher-Cunningham.
    p. cm.
  ISBN 978-0-8192-2789-8 (pbk.) -- ISBN 978-0-8192-2790-4 (ebook)
1. Food--Religious aspects--Christianity. 2. Dinners and dining--
Religious aspects--Christianity. 3. Lord's Supper. I. Title.
  BR115.N87B73 2012
  248.4'6--dc23

                          2012023814

Printed in the United States of America

for Ginger
who feeds my heart

Contents

Foreword

THE FIRST TIME I read Milton Brasher-Cunningham's recipe for strawberry shortcake, I knew he was preaching the Word. It wasn't just the intriguing idea of adding fresh chopped basil to the biscuits, but his instruction about how to do it: "A handful, I guess; I don't really measure how much."

Being a cook or a Christian is all about practice, though some would prefer it to be about rules. There are, to be sure, some bottom lines of physics and faith, as teachers from Harold McGee to St. Benedict make clear in their respective disciplines. You can't uncook a hard-cooked egg, for example, any more than you can become a monk without praying. And there are some important traditions that remain of use, whether you're following Escoffier or David Chang, the prophet Amos or the prophet Dorothy Day.

But you cannot measure your way to a perfect omelet, any more than you can study your way to grace. Beyond mastering the principles, it takes a lot of just plain doing the real thing over time: the repetitive chop and toss and sauté night after night that teaches what a "handful" means; the daily muttering over the well-worn pages of

the Psalter that teaches how to improvise a chant tone. Most skill—
and even much Wisdom, as Scripture suggests––comes through
practice. Especially, I think, the practice of failing: the broken
Hollandaise, the broken vows, the inevitable mistakes that come
when mortals attempt something that really matters.

As Milton Basher-Cunningham knows, and tells beautifully in
this book, practice isn't a solitary business. You can't have a restaurant, or a church, alone. You need to stand the heat with other
people, listen to other people weep, let other people pop fresh strawberries or little pieces of communion bread into your mouth. And
doing this takes practice, too. Sometimes you need to spatter your
sauté guy with hot grease and step on your organist's toes and say
sorry; sometimes you need to let the dishwasher teach you to poach
fish or the teenagers teach you to do scriptural exegesis and say
thank you. Always you need to cook for people you don't know, pray
for people you don't like, and eat with whoever shows up.

Of course it's not convenient. Preparing and eating meals with
other human beings is frustratingly messy and slow, whether you do
it in a home or a restaurant or a church, and the meal won't always
taste the way you expected.

But cooks and Christians know something that's far more important than convenience. Listen to the Word according to Milton
Brasher-Cunningham: *don't eat alone*. He knows, through practice,
why.

Don't eat alone, this book offers, because unexpected things
happen when you prepare food and eat with others. The same old
lunch rush with the same old fry cook can turn into a hilarious ballet
of sweaty solidarity; the same boring breakfast bowl of Cheerios
poured out for a little sister can allow a shy second-grader to share
her lunch; the same sticky sip of sweet port handed to you by the
same cranky deacon can blossom on your tongue like the crazy fruit
of a living vine, and give you the blessed nerve to pass the cup on
to a stranger.

Don't eat alone, because sharing food reveals the new thing God
is always making. In its unpredictability, a meal cooked for and eaten

with others takes us beyond ourselves, to an experience that can't be mechanically reproduced, perfectly measured, or privately managed.

Don't eat alone, because the sacrament of communion reveals how the one who came to turn over the earth, plant a vine out of Egypt, thresh grain, fill new wineskins, and break the loaves is always extravagantly feeding the whole world. How the one who shares a table with beloved friends, with gluttons and drunkards, with unwashed sinners, is always inviting everyone to partake. And so whenever we remember him as we eat with friends, or whenever we ask strangers to abide with us and break bread, he is revealed.

God feeds all living things, testifies the psalmist. *On the holy mountain the Almighty is preparing a banquet of rich foods and well-strained wine,* proclaims the prophet. *All you who are hungry, come and eat without price.* And Christ Jesus, who repeatedly calls his followers to the practice of feeding others—a little girl, a huge crowd, his sheep, himself– prepares the supper, serves the supper, and himself becomes the supper for us all. *I am the bread of life,* he says. *Take it and eat.*

We never have to eat alone again.

Sara Miles
Summer 2012, San Francisco

Acknowledgments

THE POSSIBILITY FOR this book began because Nancy Bryan sought me out after reading my blog, *Don't Eat Alone* (www.donteatalone.com). She has been everything from encourager to editor in this process and I am deeply grateful for her tenacity and support.

I learned about church in Zambia, Kenya, and Texas— all the places I grew up. As an adult, I found community in University Baptist Church in Fort Worth, Texas; Royal Lane Baptist Church in Dallas; First Congregational Church UCC of Winchester, Massachusetts; First Congregational Church UCC of Hanover, Massachusetts; North Community Church, Marshfield, Massachusetts; and Pilgrim United Church of Christ, Durham, North Carolina.

Robert Ahrens, Tim Miller, and Amy Tourniquist are the chefs who hired me to work in their kitchens. Dave Alworth, Billy Keith, and Abel Guevarra top the list of many who made it both fun and meaningful to be in the kitchen.

The list of those who have contributed and continue to add

to the conversation of how we live our lives together includes Joy Jordan-Lake, who both writes and encourages wonderfully; Burt Burleson, who is my most enduring friend; David Gentiles, whom I still miss; Billy Crockett, whose friendship birthed some great songs, moments, and memories in my life; John Brashier and our "family line" of interns; Christy de Sisto, who grew from intern to friend; Ken Hugghins, for the song title and the tamale trailer; Ken Orth, for listening well and loving whole-heartedly; Doug Aaberg, whose friendship has travelled well; Don Remick, for our days in Hanover; Gordon and Jeanene Atkinson, whose connections with Ginger and me run on multiple levels; and Nathan Brown, who shares my love for reading and writing poetry. I am also grateful for the twenty-or-so years of youth camp with UBC, Wilshire Baptist Church, and the other camps that have graced my summers over the years.

In Durham, the most encouraging city in America, I am grateful for ties to Laurabelle Sacrinity and the staff at Watts Grocery where we hang out every chance we get, to Mike Hacker and Becky de Cascio for letting me hang out on the Pie Pushers truck since I can't afford one of my own, to Sarah Vroom and Keith Shaljian and the folks at Bountiful Backyards for filling our yard with stuff we can eat and share, to Peter Katz and the Old North Durham Neighborhood Association for helping us feel at home here in our neighborhood, to Sean Lilly Wilson and the folks at Fullsteam Brewery for creating the friendliest room in Durham and for making Working Man's Lunch, to Claudia Fulshaw for encouraging me to dream, and to the growing circle of people who make it meaningful to put down roots here.

For a couple who didn't feel called to have children of our own, we are fortunate to have a bunch of folks who find their way home to our house: Eloise Parks, Jay Blackwell, Cherry Foreman, and Julie Wisnia top the list. We are also blessed with a gaggle of god-children: Ally, Julia, Samuel, Justin, and Jasmine.

My mother, Barbara, is the person most responsible for my being a cook, and she taught me how to be a fearless one, at that. I thank my father, Milton, for teaching me how to dream big and love the world. My aunt Pegi was the one who taught me what it meant to be family. I am grateful for my brother, Miller, and my sister-in-law, Ginger, for loving me through lots of stages. My nephews, Ben and Scott, feed me with new musical selections and keep me practicing my guitar. My mother-in-law, Rachel Brasher, encourages me daily. I am thankful for all the ways my father-in-law, Reuben, loved Rachel, Ginger, and me. I miss him, too.

The most persistent and dependable invitation to love in my life comes from Ginger, my wife, who somehow never loses heart. I am loved, I am loved, I am really, really, loved.

Peace,

Milton

Preface:
Come to My Window

THE DESK FROM which I do most of my writing sits in the guest room of our two-story home in front of a window that gives me a view of our backyard and the houses behind us. It is the one window in the house that doesn't have a curtain or a shade. I can always see what's out there. The last time we were in Texas to see my parents, my mother told a story about me that Ginger had never heard, which, after twenty-two years of marriage, is no easy task considering my family's propensity for repeating stories we love to tell. My family moved to Africa when I was a baby. I turned one on a ship in the middle of the Atlantic Ocean on our voyage from New York harbor to Beira in Mozambique. I lived the first years of my life in Bulawayo, Southern Rhodesia.

My room in our house had a window high above the crib that let in light but did not give me easy access to the outside. There were no screens on the window since there were no bugs to worry about. One afternoon when I was two or three, my parents put me down for a nap and decided they would lie down for a bit as well. Before too long, they heard me say, "Hi! How are you?" Mom said they smiled at each other and enjoyed the laughter in my voice. After a few moments, my father said, "Do you realize where he has to be to see outside?" With both a sense of urgency and an awareness that they didn't want to startle me such that I fell out the window, they crept around to see me perched on the window sill talking to whomever I could find.

Ginger said two things. First, she said, "I've never heard that story." Then she looked at me and said, "This explains so much." She's right. One of the things it explains is why I wrote this book.

My hunger to feel connected goes back as far as my family's stories go. I trust we were created to be community, to be "us." Come to my window; let me show you what I see.

West Trinity Avenue
Durham, North Carolina
April 2012

Introduction:
Family Dinner

AS FAR BACK as I can remember, meal time has meant a gathering together. My family ate to be together as much as we ate to be fed. Meals were markers in the day, times to talk and laugh and time to enjoy our food. We were not a perfect family, but we ate well together morning and night, left only to fend for ourselves at lunch, whether at school or at work. Breakfast and dinner, however, were not to be eaten alone. As my brother and I moved into ninth and eleventh grades respectively, and my family moved back to Texas permanently after many years as missionaries in Africa, my mother cautioned us that our lives were about to face big changes. She then asked what we wanted most to stay the same. Eating together was our reply. Dinner, as a result, became a moveable feast time-wise because it mattered. We ate early before musical rehearsal or late after ball practice, doing whatever it took to keep the feast. In my twenties, when the relationship with my family was most strained, I remember calling my parents after we had managed to reconcile beyond a particularly dark and painful stretch.

"I was afraid, sometimes," my mother said with a break in her voice, "that once we hung up the phone we might never hear from you again."

As angry as I had been in those moments she described, that thought never crossed my mind. I believe it was the years of breakfasts and dinners stacked up in my soul like pancakes that produced an unflinching tether. Things were not perfect, and (not but) we were family. We took and ate and remembered even when it hurt to do so and we stayed connected even when we did not know how.

My fascination with food led me to the kitchen at an early age;

my mother's being a ferociously fearless cook coupled with my inherent inquisitiveness meant I became a cook as well. Though we ate well together, my family was not as adept at sharing feelings around the table. My father grew up in a house where anger was the loud and common currency and he was determined for our family to be more civil and loving, which we were. I, however, internalized his good intentions as a prohibition against anger, so I didn't always know what to do with the frustration and rage that came with growing up. The kitchen was, somehow, a safe room—an open room—that let me find freedom in the smells and sounds, in the work and wonder that is cooking.

"What are you making?" I would ask my mother as I wandered in from the backyard in the late afternoon.

"Here, let me show you," she would answer most of the time, often followed days later by, "You watched me do this the other day; you do it this time."

I learned how to cook and how to teach from her. I also learned to bask in the glow of a good meal. With all the confidence of one deserving of her own cooking show, she would take a bite of what she had made for dinner and proclaim, "Isn't this wonderful?" Paula Deen has nothing on my mother. Still.

Growing up in a family with Texas roots, even though I sprouted in Africa, we called the evening meal supper. Growing up Southern Baptist, I first learned of Communion as the Lord's Supper, so it was a meal to me before it was a ritual. Supper was to be shared and enjoyed. As a child, I thought of the Lord's Supper as dinner with Jesus, in a way, with food for whoever came, much like supper was at our house. As a young Baptist boy, I gave my heart to Jesus, as we said, and took my place with him at the Table for Supper.

In Baptist life, that meal didn't come very often—usually once a quarter—for fear of being too ritualistic, as it was explained to me. But meals—good meals are rituals. We had taco salad at our house every Saturday at lunch and that didn't get old. I was youth minister at University Baptist Church in Fort Worth when I became friends with Martha, the youth minister at the Episcopal church around the corner. She explained what Communion meant to her and I began to go, regularly and quietly, to evening prayer and Mass to eat This Meal That Matters Most regularly and ritually. I learned that ritual was a good and important word that meant "meaningful repetition" rather than a term of caution, and I learned a new name: the Eucharist—the Great Thanksgiving. Coming to the Table with intention and regularity was like Saturday taco salad, something to do repetitively, joyfully, and gratefully.

"Every time you do this, remember me."

A book, then, about looking at the different meals of our lives as metaphors for Communion feels natural to me. Though it has taken many years for me to actually sit down and write it, I've collected stories and carried snippets of chapters around for years, mostly in my heart and in small scrap journals, always managing to let the days slip away without writing them down. Until now.

Thanks to the unflappable encouragement of Ginger, my wife, I pushed past my who-knows-what and wrote. The metaphors that follow are invitations to supper, if you will: ways to think about The Meal. I intend them as poetry more than prescription: jumping off places for further conversation. Hopefully, over dinner.

Signature Dish

communion

we pass the silver plate
of broken bread with
less confidence than
we pass the peace
easier perhaps to hug
than to admit our hunger
we take and eat without
a word and wait for
the wine's weaker friend
shot glasses of salvation
we place the empties
in the pew racks causing
the clicking sound of
solidarity to rattle
our hearts and shake
awake the resonance
that runs through all
the saints and suppers
that we might remember
that we might be one

M Y FIRST DATE with Ginger, who is now my wife, was a Lyle Lovett concert in a tiny club in Fort Worth, Texas. On our second date, I cooked dinner for her. It was a Saturday night and I put together a mixture of fettuccine alfredo and Cajun-spiced chicken that she thoroughly enjoyed. We fell in love with one another rather quickly, so we ate together most every Saturday night that spring and she asked for a repeat performance of the dish so often that we named it "Saturday Night Chicken." Though we do eat a variety of food, that is our signature dish: the one we most associate with us.

When people find out I have been a professional chef, they often ask, "What's your specialty?" or "What's your signature dish?" I suppose it's a fair question, though I don't think many chefs limit themselves to a particular plate other than for marketing reasons. Still, doctors and lawyers all have specific areas of expertise, so why not chefs? That said, I have never been comfortable narrowing it down to a dish or two, so I have struggled with how to answer because I didn't want to sound overly didactic ("Well, you see, that's not really how the restaurant business works") or dismissive ("I don't really think about it that way . . ."). I learned, therefore, to reframe the question in my mind by trying to hear what was behind their query, which I interpreted as asking what I most loved to cook.

I didn't go to culinary school. Instead, I came up through the ranks, starting as a dishwasher and then a prep cook, and was able to work my way up the cooking line because professional cooking is still a career where apprenticeship is an accepted and honored way to learn the craft. I started cooking for a living out of necessity.

After spending eighteen months wrestling with a severe depression that had left me unable to do much more than get up, take long walks, and write rather morose poetry, I had to do something to help make money. The hole I was digging had become more than emotional; I needed to make some sort of financial contribution to our marriage. I had worked as a minister and a teacher, but neither career offered many options. I spent a couple of weeks driving around seeing what I could figure out and then it hit me: I love to cook—maybe I could do that for a living. I found a small place that was opening and bugged the chef every day for two weeks until he capitulated and hired me. Over the next eight or nine years, I had a chance to work for and with some extremely talented and creative people who were more than willing to share their knowledge. I worked in restaurants ranging from a small breakfast place that taught me how to cook good eggs fast to fine dining restaurants where I was afforded ingredients like white truffle oil and fennel pollen. Over time, I have had a chance to refine my answer to the signature dish question, much as I had the chance to hone my cooking skills, and have come to respond in the following way:

My favorite thing to cook is comfort food. The fancy ingredients are fun, but if I can make mashed potatoes that taste so good you will leave your potatoes in your vegetable bin at home and drive to eat my cooking then I've done something special. I want to make food that makes you want to come eat with me. I want to make the kind of food that will make you remember our being together. The signature—the distinguishing mark—of a great meal is in the memory it creates.

Communion is the signature dish of our faith. Sharing the bread and the cup is at the core of who we are together. It is the meal around which we build our identity, our defining ritual.

One May evening a year or two after we moved to Durham from Boston, we sat with two friends around an iron table on the patio of La Hacienda, a Mexican restaurant in Chapel Hill, and shared an evening filled with wonderful food, frozen margaritas, friendship, laughter, and stories—all a part of our celebration of Ginger's birthday, which had several food stops along the way in keeping with our traditions. During our time in New England, one of the rituals for her birthday was a trip to the Museum of Fine Arts in Boston to wander and wonder among the paintings and then to share the cheese plate in the museum café. Though that particular item was a little out of reach on that birthday, we did end up at Six Plates, a wine bar owned by a new friend here in Durham, for their great cheese plate in order that we might keep our birthday tradition. As Ginger told of our travels from cheese plate to queso and chips, our friend Lindsey said, "Y'all are such creatures of ritual."

Yes, we are. On purpose. Ritual is best defined as "meaningful repetition"—repeating those things that help you remember, as the old saying goes, who you are and whose you are. So we end up in a Hard Rock Café on our wedding and engagement anniversaries, we chase down a good cheese plate on Ginger's birthday, and we keep repeating any number of little sayings and actions that remind us of the promises we are committed to keeping, transforming daily doings into something sacred. The repetition is a stacking of time, each experience laid one on top of the other, so that when we return to repeat it again we do so from a new perspective. All the years of cheese plates give us a different view of what it means to be together, to be alive in this world. One of my favorite Bible stories is that of Joshua telling the people of Israel to stack up the stones after they had crossed the Jordan so that in the years to come when the children asked what the stones mean they could tell the story, over and over again, of what God had done.

If ritual is meaningful repetition, habit is the opposite—repetition that grows out of convenience, compliance, or just because: unexamined repetition. Where habits grow like kudzu, rituals have to be cultivated and nourished. We have to keep stacking up stones and slicing cheese if life is going to mean something. When Jesus first passed the bread and wine, he said, "As often as you do this, remember me." One of the ways I like to interpret his words is to think he was not so much envisioning a Communion service at church as much as he was talking about mealtime in a more general sense: every time you break bread together, remember. Let all our meals be rituals and not habits.

Ginger and I married in April of 1990. Four months later, we moved from Texas to Boston. The story of how we ended up packing ourselves into a Hertz-Penske rental truck (I still can't say or write that name without shivering just a little) and driving from Fort Worth, where I had lived longer than anywhere else in my life, to make our home in the Charlestown neighborhood of Boston, which is one square mile populated by sixteen thousand people who were all anonymous to us, so we could try to start a church is a story to tell, but not right now.

About a year after that move to Boston, we purchased our first home. It was a row house—fourteen hundred square feet on four floors—that was built somewhere around 1850. It had "good bones," as our realtor liked to say, and it needed a lot of work, which we did mostly ourselves. The big project was the kitchen. Our friend J. T., a contractor with a heart of gold, was the lead on the project and I was his second. J. T. was built like a lumberjack, thought like a theologian, and worked like he was on commission. We took the room out down to the floor joists and wall studs, even taking out a dead chimney along one wall. For that, J. T. and I climbed up on the roof and dismantled the bricks above the roof line, lowering them to the ground one five-gallon bucket at a time. Then he proceeded to knock out the chimney from the top down, standing on one side and dropping the bricks down the flue where I retrieved them in the kitchen and carried them outside. He came all the way down through the middle of the house, kicking the bricks, and finally emerging in the kitchen like some sort of dust-blown Santa. The trash guys hauled off over a ton and a half of bricks when it was all over and we ended up with an extra sixteen square feet of space in our fourteen-by-ten-foot room.

I then got to design the kitchen I wanted to cook in, which meant it needed to be both a public space and one that allowed me to get my job done. We put the sink in the farthest corner of the room, with cabinets and countertops going along each wall. On one side was the stove and refrigerator; on the other side was the dishwasher along a half wall with a raised counter that faced the dining room. In the middle of the room I mounted a deep cabinet with pot drawers to serve as an island and braced it with another raised counter with bar stools where people—namely, Ginger—could sit and talk while I cooked. To complete the dining room, we found a furniture company in Boston that built new things out of old wood, so we had them build a four-by-eight table out of recovered barn wood. It filled up the room—a room that begged to be filled with people, and we did our best to comply by inviting folks to what became known as Thursday Night Dinner. The name pretty much explains it. Ginger's day off was Friday and I was at the end of a school week, so the night was relaxed for us. We invited folks whenever we got the chance and we made place cards for those who showed up. The rule became once you had a place card, you no longer needed an invitation. All you had to do was let us know by Thursday noon that you were coming and we would have a place for you. We have been married twenty-two years and still have all the place cards of everyone who has sat around our table. The rule still stands, even though we've moved to Durham.

"Works of art," said Albert Camus, "are not born in flashes of imagination, but in daily fidelity." Though I had to take those words to heart to get this book written, the truth is even more profound when I think of what it has to say about being at the table together. On any given Thursday, we had anywhere from four to fourteen people around the old farm table in our tiny urban dining room. Over time, we had a rotating group of regulars. One woman, whom we met on the street in Charlestown as she was moving into the neighborhood, was a Southern-born pharmaceutical salesperson with a wide and welcoming smile who drove all over western Massachusetts, New Hampshire, and Vermont to serve her accounts. She quit taking appointments after noon on Thursdays so she had time to get back for dinner. Around the table, we healed each other, laughed together, challenged each other, helped raise our foster daughter, listened to one another, and ate well. The bonds formed around those meals are still strong.

At the church Bible study we hold at our favorite brewery, Fullsteam (the friendliest room in Durham), we were talking one night about the stories in the Gospel of Mark, and noticing that he moves from one "immediately" to another without much regard for any kind of back-story; we wondered what he might have left out. Jesus walked up to James and John as they were getting ready to go fishing with their father and said, "Follow me," and immediately, Mark says, they dropped their nets and went. And that's all he says. No negotiation. No Zebedee fuming in the streets as his sons walked away from the family business. Jesus called. They left. Over time, I've come to think that what Mark didn't tell us was they already knew each other. Daily fidelity was at work in the building of trust and relationship. Even Zebedee knew what was coming when Jesus stopped that particular day. Mark just cut to the climactic scene.

What the gospel writers don't seem to skimp on are stories of Jesus eating. Or at least stories of Jesus and food. He eats, he feeds, he talks about food, he even calls himself the Bread of Life, and on the last night around the Table he wrapped it all up with a meal—The Meal—as the ultimate metaphor of what it means to be together. After the resurrection, he walked with the two along the Emmaus Road, talking and listening and remaining anonymous because they didn't recognize him until they sat down for dinner and the stories came alive again when he broke the bread. Even on the nights that Ginger and I sit down at the table by ourselves, I feel surrounded by the cloud of witnesses that have sat there with us all the days. I think of the hands that have touched the wood, the glasses that have been raised, all the bread broken and wine poured in our legacy of fellowship and community. It is Communion.

In my youth minister days at University Baptist Church in Fort Worth, Communion took a central place in what we did. I wanted the kids to grow up knowing more about the Lord's Supper than I had, so we shared the meal together in our mid-week youth worship even though the church only shared the meal quarterly on Sunday mornings. We also had Communion at Youth Camp, which was the centerpiece of our year together. We went off for a week with about a hundred kids and as many adults as I could get to go, and we spent the days singing and playing and hanging out and eating in Jesus' name. The closing experience on the last night of camp was Communion. We served each other in several different ways over the years and took time to talk about what we found in the meal. One year, we set up a long table in the middle of the room with several pitchers of grape juice and loaves of bread and invited people to bring someone to the Table and serve them. They began to go up in twos and threes, most going more than once; for over an hour we shared in the Great Banquet.

Somewhere in the midst of the meal, my friend Reed, who was one of the musicians for the week, invited me to eat with him. Reed was an amazing keyboard player with the self-confidence to match. His sometimes overpowering presence belied the sensitivity with which he paid attention to what was going on around him and who was there with him. We sat facing each other. He tore off a big piece of bread, held it up at eye level, and said, "You know what blows my mind, man? Everyone down through Christian history has sat at this Table. We get baptized differently, we learn about life differently, we worship differently, but we all eat here. So right now we're here with everyone who has ever been here before us and everyone who will come after us. That blows my mind." We ate and drank together and then stayed at the table, watching as kids came and went, eating and drinking and laughing and crying, a visual and visceral symbol of all that gets handed down and handed on at the Table. Like the stories in the walls of that little row house and the memories that have worked their way into the fibers of our old farm table, so the simple act of breaking bread and sharing the cup offers us the chance to see Jesus, to recognize Christ in one another, to tell our stories, and remember we always have a place to eat.

Rituals are the raw material from which we can build of our lives a mountain of memories, offering us the chance to see that we have come from God and we are going to God, that we are inextricably connected to one another by the grace of God, and, even in the scope of so grand a universe, it matters that we celebrate with our signature dishes, over and over again.

Saturday Night Chicken

1 pound boneless chicken breast, cut in thin strips
olive oil
Goya Adobo seasoning (con pimento)
Tony Chachere's Creole Seasoning
1 pound fettuccine
2 tablespoons unsalted butter
1 cup heavy cream (or 1 cup plain Greek yogurt)
1 tablespoon honey (if you are using the yogurt)
2/3 cup freshly grated parmesan cheese
salt and pepper to taste

Put a big pot of water on the stove to boil for the pasta. If you are using dry pasta, it will take longer to cook than fresh. Time it so the pasta finishes with the chicken and the alfredo sauce.

Put the chicken strips in a bowl and toss with the two seasonings. I use equal parts of each. We like it hot, so I use a good bit. Experiment to your own taste. You can also add more as you are cooking. Get a sauté pan good and hot and then add olive oil. When the oil is hot, but not smoking, add the chicken and cook until the strips are cooked through and a little crispy—about 6–8 minutes.

Melt the butter in a saucepan over medium heat and add the cream (or yogurt), stirring well. Cook until cream is simmering, but not boiling. Take some time here. The longer it cooks, the more it naturally thickens. Keep stirring. Add cheese and cook some more until the cheese is melted and well integrated into the sauce. When you add the salt and pepper, go slowly with the salt because the cheese has some already. You can also add other flavors—garlic, Cajun seasoning—to your liking. If you don't want flecks in the sauce, use white pepper.

Drain the pasta and put in a large bowl. Pour the alfredo sauce over pasta and toss. Put pasta on the plate and the chicken on top. Open a nice bottle of wine and feel the love.

Serves two with some leftovers.

Ripple Effect

daily work

The crush of afternoon traffic finds me
in an unending stream of souls staring
at the stoplight. From my seat I can see
the billboard: "Come visit the New Planetarium
You Tiny Insignificant Speck in the Universe."
When the signal changes, I follow the flow
over river and railroad yard, coming
to rest in front of our row house, to be
welcomed by our schnauzers, the only
ones who appear to notice my return.
I have been hard at work in my stream
of consciousness, but the ripples of my life
have stopped no wars, have saved no lives—
and I forgot to pick up the dry cleaning;
I am a speck who has been found wanting.
I walk the dogs down to the river and wonder
how many times I have stood at the edge
hoping to hear, "You are My Beloved Child."
Instead, I skip across life's surface to find
I am not The One You Were Looking For.
I am standing in the river of humanity
between the banks of Blessing and Despair,
with the sinking feeling that messiahs
matter most: I am supposed to change
the world and I have not done my job.
Yet. . . if I stack up the stones of my life
like an altar, I can find myself in the legacy
of Love somewhere between star and sea:
I am a Speck of Some Significance.
So say the schnauzers every time I come home.

I STARTED LISTENING TO *A Prairie Home Companion* when I was in seminary. Garrison Keillor's monologues on "The News from Lake Wobegon" taught me more about preaching than any of my seminary classes because of the way he told stories. He remains one of my story-telling heroes. He came to Durham last year without the radio show and I got to hear him in person. I remember much more of the evening, but his closing word on one story is what has stayed with me in a more disquieting way. He told us about a woman he met when he left Minnesota as a young man and moved to New York City to become a writer. They fell in love and he imagined a wonderful and successful life far away from his roots. Then came the day when she challenged him to go back. "Write about what scares you most," she said, "—that you will turn out just like them." He returned to Minnesota and found his way to writing and talking about Lake Wobegon. As he finished the story he said, "I thank her for that important slight change in my life."

I was in junior high, I think, when I first read the poem that begins,

> For want of a nail the shoe was lost.

As the poem continues, the losses mount up:

> For want of a shoe the horse was lost.
> For want of a horse the rider was lost.
> For want of a rider the battle was lost.
> For want of a battle the kingdom was lost.
> And all for the want of a horseshoe nail.

An important slight change. The oxymoron reminds us that the difference between important and slight is often difficult to discern. What seemed enormous in one moment shrinks in perspective; what seemed dispensable grows into necessity in retrospect. The bottom line is life has no discards. Each word, each motion matters because we can't see what we are setting in motion. The things we've done and the things we've left undone all qualify as important slight changes. Life is important and incidental in the same instant, as Robert Frost pointed out in "The Road Not Taken." When Frost wrote those words, he did so with an informed sense of irony. He was describing a walk in the woods that surrounded his farm north of Boston where he picked one path over another on a journey back to the barn. "And that," he wrote, "has made all the difference." I imagine him smiling as he penned those words. Sometimes a walk in the woods is a walk in the woods. Sometimes that walk brought you to the place where you wrote a poem that becomes timeless, whether or not your readers understand the irony.

When people ask how Ginger and I met, the short answer is we were at the same midwinter retreat for the Southwest Baptist Camping Group in January of 1989 at Camp Olympia. The longer version involves both of us looking back at choices we had made independent of each other such that we both ended up in Texas with ties to Royal Lane Baptist Church and on that retreat—all slight changes that grew in importance. She could have chosen to take the CPE internship in Winston-Salem and never have come to Texas. I could have scheduled something with my own youth group that weekend instead of doing the music for the retreat. I came home from the retreat and called my friend Billy to tell him the Lyle Lovett tickets I had bought for his birthday were going to be put to another use. "I met a girl," I said. Ginger still calls Billy from the venue whenever we have a chance to see Lyle. Some of the ripples to any Yes in life are those things we have to let go by, or let go of. Some of the consequences are things we cannot see. Some of the choices and promises we make have to be made over and over again for them to stay fresh and true.

In our lives together, Ginger and I have both been intentional about the important slight ways we remind each other of our love as we choose our path together day by day. I am married to the most forthright person I know; she married someone who grew up in a family that talked about their feelings once every fifteen years or so whether we needed to or not. The road I had not taken before was to learn to be immediate and specific with my feelings, particularly my anger, as she challenged me to take Jesus' admonition to not let the sun set on my wrath to heart. That important slight change taught me how to trust and be trustworthy. When we come to the Table, Paul calls us to the same slight change, saying we should not eat together until we are sure the air is clear between us. Each time we break bread together, we nourish one another with our honesty and fidelity. In a world where folks speak what they ought to say rather than what they feel, it is an important slight change.

The task of finding our place in this world in a global sense is as daunting as figuring out how to live together face-to-face. We are living in a profoundly transitional and transformational time, and it's difficult to get a sense of where we are on the map of history. Nobody who lived during what we now call the Middle Ages saw themselves as living in one of history's waiting rooms. How could they have been in the middle of anything when nothing had yet come after them? The World War that began the twentieth century didn't have a number in its name when it was fought. I dare say most everyone who has walked this earth thought they were alive at The Most Crucial Time in History.

Though Galileo and Copernicus changed how we think about our place in the universe, when we start talking about what it means to be living in these days in more existential terms, it becomes difficult to do so in a way that doesn't make us the center of the universe once more: we are going to usher in the next Reformation; we are living in the next Enlightenment. Who knows where we are. Now, in our age of informational overpopulation, not only can we not know everything there is to know, we can't even categorize or process it fast enough to keep up. When I check e-mail, the headlines on AOL read like some sort of bizarre found poem, and they change every few minutes. As I'm writing, here are the headlines:

- Drone Program Aims to "Accelerate" Use of Unmanned Aircraft by Police
- Man Attacks Noisy Child in Theater
- Inventor of the TV Remote Dies at 96
- Ancient Turtle Found to Be Massive
- Hospital Regrets Big Surgery Blunder
- Star Returning to Screen After Heartache

Beyond the news, Facebook and Twitter are conditioning us to think we need to publish almost every piece of information about ourselves. Most anywhere I turn, I am being given something else to add to the pile of stuff to know and, often, to set aside. If I'm taking a stab at where we are on the map, or at least how the world has changed while I've been walking around on it, the information overflow is at the heart of it: we are at the intersection of We Have Too Much Information and What Am I Supposed To Do With It.

The more global the discussion becomes, the smaller I tend to think. When we start talking about changing the world, I find myself thinking about the people in my kitchen, my family, my church, my neighborhood, my town. Luther drove the nail into the door at Wittenberg, it seems to me, not so much because he was intent on altering the course of global Christianity as it was because he "could do no other." It was what he needed to do that morning in that place. People like Mahatma Gandhi, Oscar Romero, Martin Luther King Jr., Rosa Parks, Nelson Mandela, and Mother Teresa were meeting the needs in front of their faces first; the universal movements that followed grew out of the particulars. Our commitment to the incidental contact of Communion is an important slight change in the fabric of the universe every time we eat and drink together. We feast on the particulars in each of our churches and connect with the cloud of witnesses who stand in an unbroken line across the ages. We feed one another in the present tense and we know we are, regardless of time, in the graceful grasp of The Love That Will Not Let Us Go.

This spring we planted dogwood and redbud trees in memory of my father-in-law, Reuben, who died last year after living with Alzheimer's. A year and a half before his death, we made the important slight change to move him and Rachel, my mother-in-law, in with us so we could help her take care of him. The move meant Rachel and Reuben left their home of forty-five years to move to a city none of us knew well. It also meant Ginger and I got to see Reuben on a daily basis. When he died, we realized one of the unforeseen consequences of his presence was that our grief was exacerbated because we were used to having him in the house. His chair still looks empty in the living room these eight months later. As the dogwood burst into bloom and the giant century-old pin oak that towers over it began to sprout leaves again, we knew spring was coming. The first spring without him. Love has let none of us go and it has given us very little in the way of what is coming next. Though each day of life might hold some sort of harbinger of what the days ahead might hold, many of the hints—on a more existential level, anyway—are not much more than, "Things are going to change," or "This is going to hurt." Life's directions are seldom any more specific than the seasonally recurring statements of the obvious offered by the dogwoods. When we look back to see where the other slight important changes we could not discern took us, we have the opportunity to make meaning of our lives in a way that gives us the eyes and ears to look and listen—and learn—and continue on. Communion, then, is a meal on the go. Whenever we share the meal, we do so in transition. We need the time together to look at one another's lives, to describe the ripples we see, and to remind one another that change is as basic to our diet as love itself.

This year I have taught a group of eighth graders whose lives stand in the middle of the intersection of unexplained change and alienation. Unconditional love is a precious and limited commodity in middle school. My class of ten is made up of kids who have not been able to thrive in a conventional classroom, so they come to our school where the classes are smaller and we can offer more concentrated attention. Some are on the Aspberger's/autism spectrum, some have ADHD or other initials to carry with them, and some were simply creative in ways that got them uninvited from their previous school. Most of them have been together for the past two years and have formed an encouraging and supportive community. The final task of our speech class was to write their personal credo. We began the project by discussing their core values and I asked them to brainstorm some statements people think are important rules for living. One of the boys, Sam, who is destined to be a scientist said, "Observe without influence." When I asked him to explain, he said when you study something in science, the goal is to study it in a way that you don't change it by your observation. I'm not a scientist, but I have read Madeleine L'Engle, who has always had a way of using the vocabulary of science to speak of faith. In *And It Was Good: Reflections on Beginnings*, she wrote,

> Quanta, the tiny subatomic particles being studied in quantum mechanics, cannot exist alone; there cannot be a quantum, for quanta exist only in relationship to each other. And they can never be studied objectively, because even to observe them is to change them. And, like the stars, they appear to be able to communicate with each other without sound or speech. . . . Surely what is true of quanta is true of the creation; it is true of quarks, it is true of human beings. We do not exist in isolation. We are part of a vast web of relationships and interrelationships which sing themselves in the ancient harmonies. Nor can we be studied objectively, because to look at us is to change us. And for us to look at anything is to change not only what we are looking at, but ourselves, too.[1]

What Sam described can't be done. We change what we observe and we are changed as the observers. *Observe*: to notice, to see, to

---

1 Wheaton, IL: H. Shaw Publishers, 2000, 20, 21.

attend to, to celebrate. I love that it is one of the verbs we use to talk about the Lord's Supper: we observe Communion. And we are changed.

In the symmetry of our universe, L'Engle's books are often on the same shelf with those of C. S. Lewis. In *Prince Caspian*, one of the Chronicles of Narnia, Lewis wrote of the children's return to Narnia. They were much older than on their previous visit. Lucy, the youngest, kept looking for Aslan, the Lion. When she finally found him, she fell on him in a full body hug.

"Welcome, child," he said.

"Aslan," said Lucy, "you're bigger."

"That is because you are older, little one," answered he.

"Not because you are?"

"I am not. But every year you grow, you will find me bigger."[2]

Observing the meal together means attending to one another and noticing how God has changed us and how God has changed in our understanding.

Change, in the restaurant world, comes in big and small varieties. Some of it is thrust upon the staff because of mistakes in delivery, equipment failure, or human inconsistencies. Some is by choice, the most significant of which is changing the menu. A couple of the places where I worked made a point of using local and seasonal ingredients, which meant the menu had to change because some items were no longer available. At some level, the changes are made in hopes of attracting new customers, though taking favorite dishes off the menu can alienate others. The question then becomes, what kind of change do we need? The question is difficult because change is not necessarily easy to invoke on an institutional level, whether it's a restaurant or a church. Yet the only way we continue to grow into God is to make change part of our credo. The better we become at observing the meal and observing

---

2 New York: Harper Collins, 1990, 141.

our life together, the more open we are to the roar of the Spirit who calls us to change our world.

What, then, passes for change? Some changes are both slight and important; others may seem large but are nothing more than repackaging. Some years ago I read an interview with Bruce Springsteen in which he said, "There's an illusion of choice that's out there, but it's an illusion, it's not real choice. I think that's true in the political arena and in pop culture, and I guess there's a certain condescension and cynicism that goes along with it—the assumption that people aren't ready for something new and different."

We, as Americans, don't do much to dispel the cynicism Springsteen articulated. We appear to be poster children for the path of least resistance, or at least the path of convenience, or the path of I'm-going-to-do-what's-good-for-me-period. I wonder if that's who we really are, or who we play on TV. We, as Christians, are called to attend to one another differently, to incarnate the important, slight changes Jesus described when he said, "I was hungry and you gave me food, I was thirsty and you gave me something to drink, I was a stranger and you welcomed me" (Matthew 25:35). The menu of faith offers us the vocabulary we need to change in ways that are nourishing and substantive: repentance, conversion, new creation. The sad irony is, in many cases, those are not the words we choose. We, as people of faith, have too often bought into the convenience and cynicism of the culture that leave us all starving and stagnating. We need more and we need to offer more to our world than the same redundant rhetoric that passes for our cultural conversation.

I'm stating the obvious; let me try it another way. We belong to a God who is the source of creation and creativity, of nourishment and nuance, of community and connectedness. We are called to love the world and to feed the world with all the resources available in the divine pantry, to let our love for God and one another ripple around the world, and with all the imagination that can grow out of our conversations, to be harbingers of hope and hospitality. When we eat and drink in Jesus' name we remember there is more than enough to go around and, until everyone is fed, we cannot be complacent.

Maple-Glazed Brussels Sprouts

This recipe is included with this chapter because one of its unforeseen ripples is that people who say they don't eat brussels sprouts will eat these.

    1/8 cup canola oil
    2 1/4 pounds brussels sprouts, halved lengthwise
    salt and freshly ground pepper
    1/2 stick unsalted butter, cut into tablespoons and
        softened
    2 tablespoons light brown sugar
    1/4 cup pure maple syrup
    1 1/2 tablespoons cider vinegar

Heat the canola oil in a very large skillet until shimmering. Add the brussels sprouts, with salt and pepper, and cook over high heat without stirring until they are browned, about 2 minutes. Add the unsalted butter and brown sugar and cook over moderately high heat, stirring occasionally, until the brown sugar is melted. Add the maple syrup and cook, stirring occasionally, until the brussels sprouts are just crisp-tender, about 7 minutes. Stir in the cider vinegar. Using a slotted spoon, transfer the brussels sprouts to a bowl. Boil the cooking liquid over high heat until thickened slightly, about 2 minutes. Pour the sauce over the brussels sprouts and serve.

Daily Bread

reflection

there are days I lay awake
at night and wonder even
worry about what's to come
because the future feels
like a past due account and
I have already spent my time
thinking about tomorrow
putting the tense in present
there are nights like this
when I fall asleep holding
on to the day like the last
bite of the meal we shared
where we passed our plates
like forgiveness and let
ourselves love and laugh
like the present were a gift
and we press our fingers
to get every last crumb
and thank God we were
made to be hungry

ONE OF MY favorite learned vocabulary words is quotidian: something recurring daily. I love it because it's an exotic sounding word that stands for an ordinary thing, but mostly I love it because it sounds (to me) like Quixote, as in Don, the Man of La Mancha. I doubt there is a real semantic connection; instead I choose not to research it and lean into the natural connection I find there.

My introduction to Don Quixote was not the novel, which I later came to love, but the musical, *Man of La Mancha*, which I saw with my family in London in 1967 on our way back to America from Africa for my parents' missionary furlough. The production we saw (I did research this) later moved to Broadway. I had no sense of who the actors were, but the characters took up residence in my heart and memory and have traveled with me since. To that point in my life, I had never seen a musical of that scale. The sets were extravagant and detailed, the costumes ornate, and the music evocative and enormous enough to fill the commodious hall to the brim with melody. Yet beyond the captivating majesty of it all was the story of magnificent defeat and unquenchable spirit.

In those days, "The Impossible Dream" was not yet fodder for lounge lizards and elevators, but was a fresh articulation of hope: "This is my quest to follow that star, no matter how hopeless, no matter how far. . . ." Then came the closing scenes where Quixote fell as the soldiers surrounded him with mirrors to force him to see a realistic and dreamless view of himself. Sancho Panza, his sidekick, was at his bedside, along with Aldonza, the prostitute Quixote saw only as Dulcinea, the lady worth fighting for. As he lay defeated, his two cohorts began to plead for his memory: "Do you remember? You must remember . . ." and they began to sing the songs and tell the tales of his glorious quotidian duties until he rose up again from his bed, thanks to his friends.

Perhaps the biggest connection between Don Quixote and daily life comes in the quixotic quest to make the quotidian meaningful. "Boredom," writes Margaret Visser, "arises from the loss of meaning, which in turn comes in part from a failure of *religio* or connectedness with one another or with one's past."[3] John Prine said it a different way in "Angel From Montgomery":

> How the hell can a person go to work every mornin'
> and come home every evenin' and have nothing to say?[4]

How does the dailiness of life move so quickly from alive to defeated, from beauty to boredom, from holy to habit? How do we incarnate the daily fidelity required to live meaningfully? "Give us this day our daily bread," Jesus taught us to pray, and perhaps with more intentional sequencing than we realize, to follow those words with "Forgive us our sins as we forgive those who sin against us"—is this a quotidian call to connectedness?

In Jesus' day, bread was a daily task, made and eaten in the same quotidian motion. Each day required the rituals of kneading and waiting and baking to meet the necessary appetites, just as we are more human when we prepare ourselves daily to forgive and to be forgiven, cleaning the slate with each sunrise.

Restaurant work is, in large parts, a sequence of quotidian tasks. At Watts Grocery, one of the restaurants where I worked in Durham, our daily bread came in the form of English muffins, which were our hamburger buns. It was often my task to make them. The recipe had several steps that required some attention. First, I mixed warm water, honey, and yeast, added some flour and then some more flour, and then eggs, oil, and salt. I let the mixture rest for twenty minutes then added more flour and let it rest again, this time until it doubled. Then I rolled out the dough, cut the muffins,

---

3 *Much Depends on Dinner* (New York: Grove Press, 1999), 20.
4 John Prine, Atlantic Records, 1971.

and let them rest another twenty minutes before I browned them on the flat top and finished cooking them in the oven.

That was not always the process. We had a handwritten recipe that went back to the opening of the restaurant and the guy who taught everyone to make the muffins. His notes provided the basic framework, but we had made changes—adjustments—as we went along, tweaking the recipe to make it work better. We had to learn how to make the recipe fit the room, taking the cooking acoustics into account, if you will, making adjustments based on the room temperature and any number of other little factors. When I first learned to make them, I was told to let the dough rest thirty minutes. When I returned to the task after several weeks of other duties, the cook who had baked the muffins in the interim told me he had learned twenty minutes made for a better muffin. And I'm sure it's changed more than once since then. Trust me.

In *Eat, Pray, Love*, Elizabeth Gilbert talks about the role ritual and metaphor play in faith. She tells the story of a Yogic saint who had a cat that wandered around and disturbed meditation. The saint tied it to a pole during the practice, a habit that became such an expectation of his followers that when the cat died (after the Yogi did), they didn't know how to meditate because the cat wasn't in place. For Gilbert, the story is a warning against becoming too tied (you'll pardon the pun, I hope) to one particular practice as the only way to do something: "Flexibility is just as essential for divinity as discipline. Your job, then, should you choose to accept it, is to keep searching for the metaphors, rituals and teachers that will help you move ever closer to divinity."[5]

The Mother Church of The First Church of Christ, Scientist is one of the most wonderful buildings in Boston. During our first years there, when many friends who had never been to Boston came to visit us, it was a regular stop on our tour of the city. On one occasion, I noticed as we entered the sanctuary that it was much brighter than it had been and I inquired of one of the docents about the change. She said that there was a crew renovating and repairing

5 *Eat, Pray, Love: One Woman's Search for Everything Across Italy, India and Indonesia* (New York: Penguin, 2006), 206.

the roof and in the process of their work they had discovered sky-lights in the dome. The lights had been painted black during World War II when many American cities on the east coast tried to darken as many windows as possible in fear that Hitler was going to send bombers. The renovation was taking place fifty years after the end of the war. People had been in the building every day of those fifty years and yet, somehow, they had forgotten what they had painted over and lost sight of more than just the skylights.

Whether a kitchen or a congregation—or any other organiza-tion—when we gather ourselves in groups we move toward codi-fying the way we do things, creating rituals and recipes to make sure we do things right. Often, I think, the things that become written in stone or scripture or on recipe cards began as meta-phors of discovery and imagination—statements of faith—but, once passed down, become statements of the status quo because perpetu-ating the institution rises higher and higher on the agenda. I'm not sure there's any way around it.

But we don't have to succumb to it.

In my daily baking of the bread, I learned again that life and faith are mixtures of all that changes and all that stays the same. I don't allow either to remain vibrant if I hold too close to the letter of the recipe, not allowing for anything new to come into the mix. When we talk about the breaking of the bread in Communion, we run into ritual and practice that has been in place for a long time. In our UCC tradition, we have more latitude to vary the way we serve the meal, so during Lent a couple of years ago, we shared the meal in a different way each Sunday. For our church, just observing Communion every Sunday was a change. After Easter, Ginger led a gathering over coffee to reflect on some of the different ways we had celebrated the Lord's Supper during Lent and the way different people had responded to the various modes. On our walk home Ginger and I continued the conversation, and it struck me that Communion also needs to be tweaked, if you will, to stay alive. Or perhaps I do better to say that I need my heart tweaked when I come to the Table, since the point is not for the congregation to adjust to me, but for me to take my place in the recipe that is my community of faith and adjust to the mix that we might make of ourselves a joyful offering to our God. At least that's what the muffins told me.

Many years ago, I saw Alan Alda interviewed by Barbara Walters in one of her first television specials and she asked about his then twenty-five-year-old marriage, commenting that bonds like that didn't hold well in the Hollywood. "How did you do it?" she asked.

"We just kept our promises," he answered. "We said we would love each other through life and we have. Everyone is looking for a custom fit in an off-the-rack world." The simplicity of the metaphor stuck with me as worth remembering. He wasn't saying just find someone and get on with it. He was saying when you decide to love, then love. Don't keep looking to find a better fit. Let the veracity of your commitment shape you. Madeleine L'Engle said a similar thing:

> Love can't be pinned down by a definition, and it certainly can't be proved, any more than anything else important in life can be proved. Love is people, is a person . . . I am slowly coming to understand with my heart as well as my head that love is not a feeling. It is a person. It has a lot to do with compassion, and with creation.[6]

It also has to do with our quotidian commitment to one another, the daily fidelity of forgiving and feeding one another. I served as a deacon in our church for a while, and we often worked on our consistency in serving the Communion elements as a means of communicating how essential the Meal was for all of us. Making sure we were lined up as we need to be, or that we were clear about who will pass what, or that we moved in some cohesive sense was not about being efficient or perfect as much as it was an expression of our intentionality and our love for the congregation. We meant to be prepared to serve and share the meal. We meant to keep our promises in our little off-the-rack church, which meant we had to

---

6 *A Circle of Quiet* (New York: HarperCollins, 1972), 43.

be able to be involved in the moment and detached enough to see what we were creating together. The specificity of our actions, like the steps to the muffin recipe, created a thin place for the Spirit to nurture and unite us.

Sacredness requires specificity. The grand esoteric themes of theology have their place, but love takes root in those specific moments when we voluntarily and intentionally enter one another's pain. "God so loved the world" makes sense when love has a name and is lying in the manger. The Incarnation (big theological concept) comes alive in the specific person of Jesus, God with us in all our off-the-rack-ness, in all our struggles, in all our, well, lives.

In the specific person of Jesus, God says "Me, too" in a way that had not been said before. The stories in the gospels are full of specifics, Jesus making particular movements, though not spectacular ones, to offer compassion and healing. He stopped when the woman with the hemorrhage touched his coat. He asked Zacchaeus if he could come over to the house. He wrote in the sand to move the focus off the adulterous woman for at least a moment. He offered Peter breakfast.

We share the bread and the cup as if our lives depend on it. Our daily bread. One of my favorite books is a little treasure called *Heidegger and a Hippo Walk Through Those Pearly Gates: Using Philosophy (and Jokes!) to Explore Life, Death, the Afterlife, and Everything in Between.* The book is a humorous and thoughtful look at philosophy, the authors deftly telling jokes to get their points across. Here is the title joke:

> So Heidegger and a hippo stroll up to the Pearly Gates and Saint Peter says, "Listen, we've only got room for one more today. So whoever of the two of you gives me the best answer to the question "What is the meaning of life?" gets to come in. And Heidegger says, "To think Being itself explicitly requires disregarding Being to the extent that it is only grounded and interpreted in terms of beings and for

beings as their ground, as in all metaphysics." But before the hippo can grunt one word, Saint Peter says to him, "Today's your lucky day, Hippy!"[7]

How do we explain God with skin on? We don't—we can't, any more than we can define love or nail down the muffin recipe. When we look at the specific brush strokes of Jesus' encounters with those around him, however, we begin to get the picture, to see what Love looks like. When we gather together at the table and participate in the simple act of passing bread and wine to one another, we remember Jesus, even as we remember who we are and why we are called to community. Love lives in the looks, the touch, the simple words of affirmation, the daily acts of recalling the promises we've made and keeping them.

Some years ago the radio program *All Things Considered* ran a series called "Sound Clips" in which they asked people to send in audio clips of meaningful or unusual sounds and then talk about what the sound was and why it was meaningful. One episode featured was the sound of glass communion cups being put in the cup holders after Communion at the Mayflower Congregational Church UCC in Oklahoma City. Vicky Werneke, who sent in the sound clip, said her pastor liked to refer to the sound as "the clicking sound of solidarity."[8]

When I was youth minister in Hanover, Massachusetts, Tom was one of the young people in our group. He was a Harry Potter look-alike with Stephen Colbert's sense of humor. He and I shared a love for odd movies. One night he brought *The Brave Little Toaster*[9] for us to watch in youth group. The story followed five appliances—a desk lamp, a small electric blanket, a vacuum cleaner, an old-fashioned radio, and the toaster—Lampy, Blanky, Kirby, No Name, and Slot Head, respectively. They lived in a cabin that was the summer home of a child whom they loved and thought of as master. He hadn't been to the cabin in a long time, so they

---

7 Thomas Cathcart and Daniel Klien (New York: Penguin, 2009), 226–227.
8 September 21, 2006, "Communion of Sound in a Church Pew," www.npr.org/templates/story/story. php?storyid=6119316.
9 VHS, directed by Jerry Rees, based on the book by Thomas Disch (Walt Disney Pictures, 1987).

decided to go to the city and find him. At some point in the story, something sacrificial was required of each member of the group to help the others and to keep them going on their journey. Though the toaster's bravery got him the marquis billing, everyone in the group made an essential contribution in one way or another. They, too, understood the sound of solidarity.

Sometimes it clicks as the cup hits the holder. Sometimes it sings in a song that carries a memory in its melody. Sometimes it whispers in a word of encouragement or connection. Sometimes it travels silently in a touch or an act of hopeful sacrifice. However it comes, it, too, requires specificity. I don't hear the word without thinking of Lech Walesa and the Solidarity Worker's Union in Poland, whose uprising in the summer of 1980 led to the overthrow of the Communist government there and contributed to the dissolution of Soviet control in Eastern Europe. They stood together and changed the world. In more recent days we have seen the same solidarity in various countries throughout North Africa and the Middle East. Walesa said, "The thing that lies at the foundation of positive change, the way I see it, is service to a fellow human being." He was awarded the Nobel Peace Prize in 1983.

Most of the noise in our world these days is divisive: we are labeled red or blue, black or white, right or left, right or wrong, us or them. War has become the descriptive metaphor of choice for the media. But listen—listen to the strain of hope underneath the cacophony of chaos. Listen to the daily fidelity that is marked by all those who get up every day and keep their promises. Hear the quotidian rhythm that is essential to the recipe for our connectedness. You can hear it in the clink of a cup or the word of a friend, in the bold marching of an earnest throng and the small gathering of people coming together to create a memory. It infuses life in everything from communion cups to small appliances, youth groups to labor movements.

This is the day that our God has made; let us rejoice and be glad in it.

Refrigerator Rolls

(This is an old family recipe that is the bread of choice at our house.)

> 1 quart milk, scalded and poured over
> 1 cup sugar and
> 1 cup butter

(I do it in the bowl of my KitchenAid mixer on low speed.)

Let cool and then add

> 2 packages yeast dissolved in
> 1/2 cup water

Add

> 8 cups of flour, one cup at a time
>   (I use 1 cup of whole wheat flour.)
> Cover and let rise until doubled, then add
> 1 cup flour mixed with
> 3 teaspoons salt
> 2 teaspoons baking powder
> 1 teaspoon baking soda
> Cover and let rise again.

When I make our rolls, I use a two-inch biscuit cutter and then drag the bottom of the rolls through some olive oil and fold them in half. I then place them in either a baking dish or a rimmed baking sheet, depending on how many rolls I want to make. Bake at 425 degrees for 12–15 minutes. The recipe will make about four dozen rolls. You can bake the dough in loaves; it also makes great cinnamon rolls. We're talking seriously addictive bread here.

Cooking Line

thirty-seven times

Abel spent the afternoon
prepping the plate:
slicing shiitakes and scallions,
reducing the risotto,
spreading the mixture on
sheet pans to cool.
I formed the rice balls and
rolled them in panko;
he cut sweet potatoes,
blanched greens, and
roasted garlic to make
the cream sauce.
Thirty-seven people
ordered the dish and received
a visual and culinary treat:
the stack of sweet potatoes
on the sauté of spinach;
the saddle of sauce set
to bed the three golden-
crusted arancini;
the last ladle of cream
dropped like a blanket
across the top—and
a sprinkle of scallions.
Only those relegated to
the kitchen were fortunate
enough to see the tenderness
in Abel's hands as he
nestled the small orbs
as though they were as fragile
as they were flavorful;
the affection with which
he baptized them in the
purée of garlic and goat cheese;
or the sumptuous smile that sent
the dish on its way. Thirty-seven times.

I N OUR *FOOD Network* world, being a chef has become asso-
ciated with being a celebrity. The job looks glamorous and
challenging—and it can be both—but you hardly see anyone
break a sweat or get very messy except in the course of an *Iron Chef*
smackdown. In the daily fidelity of a working restaurant kitchen,
the cooks are both talented and tired. It's hard work. There are
moments of brilliance, perhaps even whole evenings, but it is still
manual labor from hauling twenty-five-pound bags of flour to
butchering meat to dicing pounds and pounds of onions, celery, and
carrots for soups and stocks.

For most line cooks the shift starts three or four hours before the
restaurant doors open, and most every one of those minutes matters. The prep list is a combination of things that have to be done
to prepare for the day's impending meal and things that must be
done to prepare for the meals to come. On most any afternoon, as
the cooks slice vegetables and trim meat, there is at least one pot
on the back of the stove filled with stock simmering for later use.
These stocks are the basis for most all of the soups and sauces that
will come along. The back story, if you will. And they take time.
Good chicken stock means roasting the chicken bones for an hour
or so until they are browned, deglazing the roasting pan with white
wine, and then scraping everything into the stock pot. The *mire-
poix*—the kitchen's "holy trinity" of onions, celery, and carrots—are
rough chopped (after the onions are peeled, of course) and roasted
as well for about thirty minutes and then they are added to the pot,
along with some garlic, fresh herbs, and peppercorns. The pot is
then filled with water and brought to a boil. Once it boils, the cook

lowers the heat to a slow simmer, with only one or two bubbles coming to the top occasionally, and it is left uncovered to reduce over several hours. The final steps are to strain and cool it. Six or eight hours of work and attention go into making one of the building blocks of any number of recipes and something that gets used up quickly. But no one serves chicken stock. It is, as I said, the back story. When it's done right, it changes everything, and doing it right means taking time, which doesn't come easy in our drive-through world.

The back story. In *Like Water for Chocolate*,[10] Laura Esquivel illustrated the significance of every element of a dish—the feelings along with the ingredients. In one scene, the woman making the beans is bitterly angry and everyone ends up nauseated. In another, the same woman, this time full of love, makes dinner and everyone pairs off and heads for the bushes with more simmering than just the stock pot.

The First Congregational Church UCC of Hanover, Massachusetts was blessed to have had a secretary named Doris, who was one of the kindest people I have ever known. She was a lifelong member of the church and knew the members better than the pastors did. If I needed a back story, I asked her. Doris was also responsible for helping to carry on a couple of the church's long-standing and most meaningful rituals. On Ash Wednesday, she baked cross-shaped loaves that she then sliced in such a way that they did not lose their shape, yet people could easily pick up a piece of bread when they came to the altar for Communion. You could taste her love and devotion. Every meal that matters has a back story, a story of preparation, a story of how things came together to make the moment.

When I lived in Massachusetts, many of the restaurant workers were Brazilian, so I did my best to pick up a little kitchen Portuguese. My favorite dishwasher was a man named Pedro who looked like a Brazilian Mr. Miagi. He was short, tenacious, and unflappable in his happiness regardless of how the dishes stacked up. Our chef,

---

10 *Like Water for Chocolate: A Novel in Monthly Installments with Recipes, Romances, and Home Remedies,* trans. Thomas and Carol Christensen (New York: Doubleday, 1992).

Robert, who was passionate and boisterous, had a habit of bellowing, "Obrigado too much" when he wanted to say thank you—a habit that became a ritual for us all. Monday nights were my night alone on the line because it was usually slow; Pedro was the only one in the dish room. One evening he brought me a stack of sauté pans and I gave the appropriate expression of gratitude to which he responded, "You're welcome, Cibolla," with a hearty laugh. I was puzzled and it must have shown on my face because he explained. "In Portuguese, tomato is *tomache*. Onion is *cibolla*. You say, 'Thank you, Tomato,' and I say, 'You're welcome, Onion.'" Thus was a second line added to our litany of thanksgiving.

In North Carolina, most of the folks in the kitchen are Spanish speakers. My favorite kitchen pun was lost on them, as was most of my kitchen Portuguese vocabulary. When I worked at the Faculty Commons at Duke, Abel was my most frequent cooking partner on the line and Tony was the dishwasher. Abel was a teacher before he was a cook and loves learning on either side of the equation. He is a five-foot-four bundle of enthusiasm and inquisitiveness. Tony became my new favorite because of his gentle spirit and his indefatigable work ethic; when the line got busy he also became a cook in training. When Abel was there, everything went smoothly because he could direct Tony, but Abel didn't work every night. On his nights off, I was left to guide Tony and he spoke less English than I did Spanish, so trying to teach him to make the dishes in the heat of the dinner rush was its own challenge, to say the least. What I needed most was for the dishes to be done well; for Tony, what appeared to matter most was to show how quickly he could apply his newly acquired knowledge.

One afternoon before Abel left, I asked, "How do I say 'wait' in Spanish?"

"Espera," he answered.

Espera. The word was easy to remember not only because I said it repeatedly over the course of the evening, but also because it sounded like a word I knew: *esperanza.* Hope.

Again, who knows if the words are related etymologically, still the resonance is audible. We must wait to get ready, wait to listen well, wait to be prepared, wait to understand, wait in order that we might find hope. Expedience is not the path to *esperanza*.

Hope, like good stock, takes time. It needs room to learn and season, to reduce to its essential quality. Faith cannot find its flavor in an instant any more than Tony could get it right the first time or the stock could be done in an hour. We have to take time to learn.

When I moved from prep cook to the line at the Tamarind Tea House, my first cooking job, I needed to know how to cook eggs well, and quickly, because it was a breakfast place. My mentor was a guy named Kevin who had spent his kitchen career in diners and breakfast joints, and he was good at breakfast. He was in his early thirties and already had fifteen years in the kitchen. He was thin and weathered—more by his smoking and the years over the stove than by the sun—and he had Irish red hair that had a mind of its own. The only thing more unbridled than his spirit was his language. And he could cook. During my training shifts, I watched him circle the bottom of the egg pan with just enough olive oil to make them not stick, crack the eggs with one hand and then, at just the right moment, pick up the pan and flip the eggs with a gentle flick of the wrist. He could keep three or four pans going at once. After the shift, I asked him how I could learn to flip eggs. He walked over to the reach-in refrigerator and pulled out a flat of thirty eggs. He set them down on the table beside the stove, pulled down a stack of pans, and said, "The only way to learn is to break some eggs. By the time you get to the end of the flat, you'll be an egg man." He was right. Learning costs time, persistence, and patience. And a few eggs.

Espera. Wait. *Esperanza*. Hope.

When we come to the Table in Communion we are called to take time to be together. The Eucharist ought not have an express lane. It takes time: time to serve the elements of The Meal, time to stand in line, time to think and pray, time to prepare to eat together, and time to remember how we got here. I remember an article in

Texas Monthly when I was in seminary that focused on the pastor of a megachurch in Houston. He bragged about the amount of money the church had spent on facilities and the extravagance of his office suite, but what got me even more was the pride he took in how quickly the deacons in his church could serve the Lord's Supper. They had found a company that made a disposable plastic cup with a lip on one side that cradled a morsel of bread so both elements could be handed out together. "We can serve three thousand people in less than four minutes," he said, as if that were a good thing. *Espera.* That's no way to eat a meal. We need time to be together, to eat together, to take stock of what has transpired since our last gathering. The Body of Christ is not fast food. Too much depends on the Supper to eat on the run and not take time to tell our stories.

Part of my story on the cooking line is that twice in my career I ended up without a job for reasons other than my choosing to leave. The last time it happened, I decided to make a cold call on the restaurant across the parking lot from the unemployment office (excuse me—the career center) in Plymouth, Massachusetts. It was a funky little place called RooBar with a really cool menu. I met the manager and we had a nice conversation. He took my résumé and then called me about an hour later to say I should call the chef, Tim, at home, which I did. In the course of the conversation, he asked, "Are you self-taught?"

"Yes," I answered, meaning I had not gone to culinary school but had learned in the kitchen. Tim had trained at the Culinary Institute of America (CIA), but he went on to talk about how most all of the folks in his kitchen were self-taught—and most of them had been with him five or six years. He also talked about how he enjoyed training and teaching people, which was true. Tim ran the most efficient and consistent kitchen I've ever worked in and he did it without being a taskmaster or losing his joy for cooking. I learned a great deal from him, even though I only got to work there for a short time before we moved to Durham. That evening after our conversation, however, I wished I had been able to go back and answer differently. I'll do it now, instead. I'm not self-taught. I apprenticed. I've been taught by everyone I've worked with.

- Joao taught me how to make Brazilian sweet potato salad.
- Carlos taught me how to make soups.
- Kevin taught me how to flip eggs.
- Sunichi taught me how to make maki rolls.
- Eric taught me how to make a beurre blanc.
- Jason taught me how to make chicken Marsala.
- Bill taught me how to test how well a steak is done.
- Gigi taught me how to use the fry-o-lator.
- Jose taught me how to run the big dishwasher.
- Alfonso taught me how to cut fruit with flair.
- Pedro taught me how to make mashed potatoes for three hundred.
- Robert taught me how to run a kitchen.
- Tim taught me how to make focaccia.
- Dave taught me how to make collard greens.
- Abel taught me how to make a rosemary cream sauce.
- Mom taught me how to make fried chicken.

Hardly a week went by in the kitchen that I didn't learn something that helped me grow as a chef or explained something I was learning by experience. It's one of the reasons I love working the line in the kitchen, because it is where knowledge and skills are handed down and passed along. The point of working together was to teach and to learn, to listen and to practice, to become a better team. No one on the line cooked in solitary. For the dishes to be consistent, excellent, and to come out at the same time on each order, we all had to be willing to learn and to share what we knew. Most of us are not a part of preparing the elements of Communion, so when we come for The Meal, we come to eat, not to cook. But life is like the cooking line in the sense that, if we are to understand why our togetherness is so crucial to the vitality of our faith, we must all come to terms with the fact that none of us is self-taught.

For a time we had both a New York strip steak (about 10–11 ounces) and a pork tenderloin (6–7 ounces) on our menu at Watts Grocery.

Both pieces of meat were cooked on the grill—and the pork took twice as long to cook. Every time. I was talking about it with Alan with whom I was working a catering event. Alan has been cooking for thirty years. He is so Italian that he looked like he had come from Central Casting. He loved to talk and teach and delivered his lessons with a wonderful balance of swagger and compassion. "You know why it is that the pork takes longer, don't you?" His question didn't wait for my answer. "The steak is cut off the whole strip, so the grain is exposed. The tenderloin is cut in half, so the grain remains intact. The heat can pull the moisture out of the steak, so it cooks quickly; the grain of the meat insulates the pork, so it takes longer." I understood. Individual steaks were cut off a much larger piece of meat, slicing across the strip and exposing the grain. The pork tenderloins were about a pound apiece; one diagonal cut gave us two servings. I had already moved to metaphor before he finished the lesson.

Life butchers us all. We all share in the experiences that cut across the grain and leave us exposed: grief, fear, change, tragedy. But things aren't that clear-cut. For some, the death of a loved one opens them up to the world like a surgical procedure, leaving them feeling lonely and vulnerable, but open nonetheless. Grief causes others to insulate themselves. It's not a question of right or wrong any more than the beef is superior to the pork. You can't force the latter folks to open up any more than you can successfully cook a pork tenderloin by cutting it into small pieces so it will grill faster. All you will end up with are little porcine hockey pucks and hardened hearts. The pork needs the insulation to cook well because it needs the time. The point is to listen and learn from one another so we come through it together. We, as the Body of Christ, are called to feed one another, both literally and spiritually, and to prepare one another to feed the world. Some of us are ready, some have been burned, some still need some time. All of us have a place at the Table for every meal.

Some years ago, Ginger and I were walking through Davis Square in Somerville, Massachusetts, when a homeless man yelled out from his seat on the sidewalk, "Change!"

Ginger turned and said, "Sorry, I don't have any money;" simultaneously, I blurted, "I'm trying, I'm trying."

The two uses of the word aren't that far apart, I suppose. Change, on the one hand, has to do with how you break down a dollar bill— or a five, or a ten—into smaller pieces: four quarters; ten dimes; two quarters, three dimes, three nickels, and five pennies. On the other hand, change also has to do with how we break down the bigger picture and figure out the new recipe for how to make things work, as familiar faces move away and new ones appear. Stability, if not overrated, is certainly over-expected. Life is made of change. Our lives are dynamic, not static. There is no way to stand still, to stay the same. We are dynamic creatures created to negotiate this changing thing called life.

In restaurants that serve more than one meal, change is a constant and every member of the staff depends on the kindness of coworkers to leave their stations in shape for those who follow. Each is expected to leave things ready for the next shift to come in, which means everything from cleaning well to leaving notes about what might have been used up or will need to be prepped, to taking time to refill squeeze bottles or consolidate the produce in the walk-in refrigerator. Life outside the kitchen is no different. Whatever the action or the situation, we are, for the most part, following someone into that situation and will be followed by someone else, whether we're talking about grocery lines or church halls. Think about who will be walking into the room next, pulling into the parking place next, using that shopping cart next, stepping into your spot once you have moved on. I'm not advocating Random Acts of Kindness (though I like those) as much as making a case for Intentional Acts of I Knew You Were Coming After Me. In the midst of change, we need to do all we can to let one another know who and what we can depend on. Communion is a visceral reminder that we are all being followed, even as we follow those who have come before us. We may not be able to control much of the situations we walk into, yet we can determine how we will leave things when we depart.

Change is a part of the fabric of our human existence. We eat the same meal at Communion each time and yet it is not exactly the same because some who were there before have gone and others have joined the circle. We bring new joys and sorrows along with new understandings of how we live with our losses. We have new questions, new hopes, new hungers even as we yearn for new perspectives on things that continue to eat at us. Wait and hope. Come and learn. Take and eat.

Open-Faced Chicken Pot Pie

(This is one of our standards at Upstairs at the Commons, the restaurant at Duke.)

Cheddar Biscuits

> 2 cups flour
> 1 tablespoon baking powder
> 1 tablespoon salt
> 2 tablespoons oil (or shortening)
> 3/4 cup grated cheddar cheese
> 1 cup buttermilk

Mix dry ingredients; add oil (or cut in shortening) until it is a coarse meal; add cheese. Work into a ball and cut into 3-inch rounds. Bake at 450 degrees for 10–12 minutes.

Chicken-Vegetable Filling
(This is what I put in—the recipe is very adaptable to what you like.)

> 2 tablespoons olive oil
> salt and pepper
> 1 pound boneless chicken breasts, cut into small
>   pieces
> 1/4 pound prosciutto, cut in small strips
> 4 scallions, cut in 1-inch lengths
> 1 medium carrot, diced
> 1 medium potato, diced

2 cups green beans, trimmed and cut into
   1-inch pieces
1 tablespoon chopped fresh thyme leaves
1/2 cup chicken broth
cayenne pepper
1/4 cup sherry
1 cup heavy cream

Heat oil, add chicken and salt and pepper, and cook till browned (about 8 minutes); add prosciutto and cook one more minute. Reserve.

In same skillet, heat chicken broth and add scallions, carrots, potato, and green beans; bring to a boil and let cook until broth is almost evaporated. Add thyme, cayenne, and chicken, and cook everything over medium heat for 1 minute.

Add sherry and cook about 2 minutes, until almost evaporated; add cream and simmer until slightly thickened—about 5 minutes.

Split the biscuits. Put bottom halves on plates (I like to use large bowls), spoon chicken mixture on top, and then add biscuit tops. Serves four.

Soup Kitchen

shelter

I talked to one guy today
who got tired of construction
and "making the wrong people
rich," which was as far as he got
before another guy who
used to work with an autistic
kid, asked me to help him out—
together we were cooking
breakfast for folks at the shelter
who stood single file to get
sausage, oatmeal, and eggs.
Taciturn, they took their trays,
and I wondered what unspoken
gospels were going by—
the dishwasher in shirt and tie . . .
the baby in the stroller . . .
the volunteer who could not
speak and growled with a smile
through his clenched teeth . . .
the four men in the corner
who ate without a word . . .
the woman serving coffee.

I stood in the middle of
the used book store of life,
where worn copies of great
works seem to be stacked
to go unnoticed, put where
they might remain unread;
the roomful of remainders
remained since lunch was served.
"The rice was a little
undercooked,"
said one, kindly, "but I loved
the concept of the meal."
Me, too. I love a table
big enough for food critics
and failures, architects and
addicts, teachers and
turncoats, homeless,
hopeful, left out, left over,
betrayers and betrayed—
where—for a few moments—
every last book on the shelf
is dusted off long enough
to be recognized and read.

As youth minister at University Baptist Church in Fort Worth, I took our students on a mission trip to Chicago in the spring of 1990 to work with the folks at Uptown Baptist Church who were doing wonderful things to reach out to the neighborhoods around them. Uptown Chicago, in those days, was an historic yet largely forgotten part of town full of people who needed help. We went to help with small construction projects, tutoring, clean up, and whatever else they needed us to do; we went so our young people could see a larger world than the one we lived in. A couple of weeks before the trip, one of the parents made an appointment to talk to me. His daughter, who was a leader in the group, was not signed up for the trip and he wanted to come and tell me why. He talked about the expense of the trip, which I was able to answer, and then he said, "I guess I'm just scared she's going to come back and decide to be a missionary or move away and try and change the world."

"I can see how that's scary," I said, "because that's what I hope happens."

Uptown Church had all kinds of ministries aimed at meeting the needs in front of them, not the least of which was a community meal. Twice a week they prepared and served food for the neighborhood. Two things made it significantly different than any other soup kitchen environment I had known. First, no one stood in line. Every table had a tablecloth and a place setting and the guests, as we called them, were invited to sit down and we served the food at the tables. Once we had served the meal, we were encouraged to get a plate of our own and join them for dinner so we could hear their stories and learn more about who had come to dinner. The second thing was the meal was open to whoever wanted to come and eat. Many came because they were hungry and had no money for food; others were there because they hungered for community. After serving dinner one night, I sat down next to a man wearing what looked to me to be a rather expensive suit. No one else at the table was dressed like him. He said he came to eat at Uptown at least every other week. He worked as a broker on the commodities exchange. "If I don't come here, it's too easy to let myself believe everyone lives like I do." He knew the people at his table by name.

Uptown, like anywhere offering a community meal, worked on a budget. I suppose that's how shelter meals got labeled as soup kitchens to begin with, since soup can be inexpensive, made out of leftovers and whatever is on hand. When I worked at the restaurants in Durham, one of the things I enjoyed most was making the soup. For our lunch buffet at the Faculty Commons, we served two soups (one vegetarian) and the selections changed daily. Fridays meant New England clam chowder, but the rest of the week was wide open. At Watts Grocery, we always had a soup of the day. In either place, I relished the chance to be the soup maker. One of the reasons I loved it was it gave me the chance to be creative. I took stock of what was in the walk-in, what was plentiful, what needed to be used up, or what we needed to complement the menu—and created the soup. I got to be pretty good at it.

Soup is the main event at Empty Bowls, a fundraiser for Urban Ministries of Durham (UMD), one of our emergency shelters. It is one of my favorite events in our city. The idea is cool. Thirty bucks buys you a handmade ceramic bowl and a ticket to a room ringed with soup offerings from local restaurants. You can fill your bowl as many times as you like and then vote for your favorite—with dollar bills. UMD serves about seven hundred and fifty meals a day to those most in need in our town. For three years I got to be one of the soup makers for the event. The first time I participated, I asked Ginger which soup I would make and she said, "Make the corn chowder."

The challenge of making soup for Empty Bowls was making ten gallons of it, which meant I had to rethink my quantities. What I did know was I needed corn, onions, celery, potatoes, red peppers, roasted jalapenos, black beans, vegetable stock, cream, and cumin. A soup needs some time to come together, so I worked over a couple of days. The first afternoon I peeled enough potatoes to fill two five-gallon containers, cut a whole case of corn off the cob and soaked the beans. Then I made a big pot of vegetable stock, including the corn cobs to sweeten it up a bit. The next day I diced celery and potatoes, cooked the beans, and began to bring things together. As I told Abel about the event and the soup I was making, he began to wave his hand as if to stop me.

"My sister, she makes this soup. This is a very important soup. It is not easy to make." He began to describe how her sister created her soup and then he said, "You know not just anyone can make this soup. It is a special soup. My sister, she says if an angry person is around her when she is making this soup, then it will break. Sometimes she and my mother say no one can come around while they are making this soup so that no one will ruin it." Abel talked a lot about his sister's cooking. He is from a family of cooks, yet when his family wanted to feel most like family, she was the one who took over in the kitchen. He always beamed when he talked about her. We laughed and told family cooking stories as the soup simmered, adding all the emotion we could to our offering.

You build a soup the way you build a life, I suppose, tweaking ingredients as you go, changing the recipe, and adding in the flavors around you. What Abel's sister knew was some of the flavors added themselves, so one had to be mindful of what or who gets near the pot. In the kitchen at the Commons, some of the flavoring was done by Billy, the daytime chef, who was a cross between Barney Fife and Eddie Murphy; Mauricio, Abel's nephew, who was equally good at smiling and working hard; Jorge, our resilient daytime dishwasher who sang his way through every shift; Abel; Tony, who worked hard to soak up everything around him as he washed and cleaned; and me. We made good soup.

When Paul gives instructions for sharing the eucharistic meal, he admonishes us to make sure our hearts are clear and we have asked for and offered forgiveness. If someone is angry or bitter or resentful, it spoils the food. If something is wrong between us, we must go and set it right and then come back to the table, rather than let it poison the meal because the Supper is more than a simple stop along the way or even a ritual worth repeating; the meal is The Point. If we can't come to the table together, then we can't come together.

One of my greatest soup hits is one I do have a recipe for: Uncle Milty's Guinness and Chocolate Chili. I made it with some regularity at Duke, particularly in the winter. When it was on the menu, Billy made a point of making sure there was a little left to take home. One night as we prepared to leave, he said, "I'm taking home some of that damn good chili, Milt. That's my supper: a grilled cheese and this damn chili. And then I'm gonna take a nap." As he was ladling the chili into a container he said, "What's your wife's name—Ginger?" answering his own question. "I'll bet that's why she married you, Milt. You made chili and she said, 'Damn, I can't let this guy go.'" And he let loose a laugh that improved all the soups in a ten-mile radius.

If Jesus had lived in a time when consistent and easy heat was available, I think we might serve soup for communion along with the bread and wine. The beauty of filling bowls from one shared pot, of making a meal of what we have on hand, and eating something that is a little messy and undignified is a perfect fit. One loaf, one cup—and one big pot.

My other contact with Urban Ministries occurs four or five times a year when our church volunteers to cook dinner at their site. UMD has a staff that cooks breakfast and lunch every day, but they rely on various groups to provide dinner. We have a dedicated group of Pilgrims (as we call ourselves since we are Pilgrim United Church of Christ) who show up every time there are five Tuesdays in a month. One crew comes in around four o'clock to prep and cook and the other crew comes in about six-thirty to serve the meal.

The menu is ours to both create and prepare and we work hard to make sure it's tasty, nutritious, and plentiful. We don't have one set meal that we repeat, though we do have a rotating group of favorites. Whatever the menu for the evening, we work hard and fast to make our offering to the two hundred and fifty plus people who stand in line for supper. Because of my background and experience working with large amounts of food and the fact that I'd rather be in the kitchen than most anywhere else, I'm on the cooking crew. It is an exercise in faith and imagination—good partners, under the circumstances, because none of my recipes was written for three hundred people. I know the ingredients and the basic proportions, so it's a matter of working until the taste and texture are right. Cooking is, after all, improvisational theater.

The kitchen at UMD is well used and rather worn. The room is clean and well kept, but many of the appliances are tired and the shelves made to hold the pots and pans not as well populated as they need to be for the size of the crowd. The subsistence budget means even staples like salt and pepper are not a guarantee. We have learned over time that we need to bring most everything with us, just as we have learned to buy enough of those kinds of basics to leave some behind as well. We are able to pay for the meal because of the children of our church. The first Sunday of the month, which is our Communion Sunday, is also known as "Penny Sunday." When the children come forward for their time with Carla, our minister of education, they receive baskets and then move out among the congregation as we well-trained adults pull out sandwich bags of pocket change and do our best to equitably distribute them among the smiling passers-by who then take it all back to the altar for us. Both children and adults take the offering very seriously. As we share the Eucharist, the baskets are stacked in front of the altar, reminding us of whom we are feeding even as we are being fed. Those pennies and dimes and quarters add up to more than enough for us to be able to make a real home-cooked meal for the people who stand in line for dinner every Fifth Tuesday.

At Urban Ministries the people stand in line to get their meals. I

often think about the servers and tablecloths at Uptown and wonder
what we can do from behind the steam tables at UMD to offer
some dignity along with dinner. Having everyone sit down first is
not the only option. Finding a way to humanize those who come
for help is. We are not serving meals, we are serving people. The
direct object makes a difference. When we stand in line to take our
place at the altar to be fed, we come with our own needs and emer-
gencies. We need someone to look us in the eye and say, "This is
the Body of Christ," as if those words mattered more than anything
else. We need to hear our names called. We need to know dinner
was made for us. For all of us.

I love to sing harmony. As a result, I love gospel music. When I
was in high school, my brother and I would race home from church
in Houston so we could watch *Gospel Jubilee*, an hour-long parade
of old time gospel quartets. Sometimes on Sunday nights we would
talk the church pianist into staying late so we could sing our way
through some of the old standards. Nothing beats a good tenor line.
Harmonies are also why I love bluegrass music: it's gospel music
with guitar, fiddle, and mandolin. Though I can get lost in the
music, the theology trips me up sometimes. One of my favorite
songs to sing is:

> this world is not my home I'm just a passing through
>
> my treasure's all laid up somewhere beyond the blue
>
> the angels beckon me from heaven's open door
>
> and I can't feel at home in this world anymore

I know these old songs grew out of times of hardship, yet I have
to wonder why escape felt like the most hopeful choice. Whatever
eternity looks like, I trust being in the unfiltered presence of God
will be worth the trip *and*—not but—this world is my home and I

think God expects more of me than to wish I were somewhere else, even if I sound good wishing it.

Wishing and hoping aren't the same thing. Urban Ministries has been in Durham for nearly three decades. They have done a great job serving our community and widening the circle of those who come to help and feed those in need. Still, today there are more people in need than there were in 1983. Doesn't that require of us, the people of God, to see this world as our home? We are called to be God's people and were made to walk on this planet to love one another and to feed one another in the face of whatever life brings us.

We stand in line for communion when we share it by intinction, which means folks come forward, take a piece of the bread, dip it in the cup, and then eat both elements together. The practice was new to me when I joined the UCC, and I struggled with it because it felt like it was motivated by expediency. I kept seeing images of the Texas pastor bragging about how quickly they served everyone. I did some research and found the practice took hold in American churches during the tuberculosis scare at the beginning of the last century. People were afraid to pass plates or drink from a common cup, so churches worked to find a way through the fears and back to the meal. What I interpreted as a short cut was a sincere attempt to stay true. When we line up for our meal together, we look like a Depression-era photograph of people waiting in a soup line— and not so different from our Fifth Tuesday friends. In our sacred soup line, some stand racked with grief so fresh they have a hard time sitting in worship, some struggle with chronic pain, some have physical ailments, and a host of others bear scars and heartaches that are not quite as apparent, all of us in line with every one of the walking wounded of the faith who have come before us and all those who will follow us, not because the bread and the cup offer a quick solution to the things we carry with us, but because we are not alone and there is enough to sustain us beyond our fears, failures, words, and hunger.

One of the sentences that lives deep in my memory and rises to the surface is from the liner notes of a friend's record from so many years ago that it actually was a record: "Thanks to God, the Ultimate Spendthrift."

Spendthrift: a person who spends possessions or money extravagantly or wastefully; prodigal. Perhaps, it's a stretch to think of the words *wastefully* and *prodigal* as descriptive of God, but then again look at the extravagance of a sunset or an iris or a bluebird. Whether as individuals or institutions, we are pointed towards self-preservation, yet we belong to a God who is not a save-it-for-a-rainy-day kind of God. When the one we call the Rich Young Ruler came to Jesus and asked what it would take to follow him, Jesus looked at him (and loved him, the gospel account says) and then told him to give away everything he had and come along for the ride, to be a spendthrift. He couldn't do it.

I was a part of a discussion at our church around how many cups we needed to fill for Communion one Sunday. The question was asked in the spirit of not wanting to be wasteful. I couldn't see past the possibility that someone would reach for a cup and there wouldn't be one because we had been too cautious. As I am wont to do, I moved to metaphor. For me, the fuller the tray, the better the image. When we serve people at UMD, we make a point of having enough for seconds and we always try to leave leftovers. How I wish we came to the altar expecting to eat more than a small hint of bread. What if we came around for seconds: we have plenty, come and eat again. Drink one. Drink two or three or seven. There's enough to go around and then some, because we belong to God.

Uncle Milty's Guinness and Chocolate Chili

    2 pounds ground beef
    1 onion, diced
    1 large can (29–30 ounces) red beans
    1 can Guinness
    1 ounce unsweetened chocolate (fair trade)
    diced green chiles or jalapeños
    cumin
    dark chile powder
    salt and pepper

In a large pot, sauté the beef and the onion until beef is cooked through; drain the fat and leave meat and onion in the pot. Add beans, Guinness, chocolate and heat until simmering. I didn't put amounts on the peppers and spices because you may like it less hot than I. The green chiles are milder than the jalapeños (I use canned in both cases); the cumin won't add heat, but gives it a kind of smoky flavor. I have also ground up dried ancho chiles into a powder and added them instead of the dark chile powder. The stout and the chocolate give the chili a sweet undertone alongside the savory cumin and the peppers. This is good stuff.

Serves 8–10.

Mile Markers

keepsake

there are some nights
when the sky turns
the color of friendship
and fades into the crisp
darkness of gratitude
we ate with friends
drank and talked as well
and then walked away
dropping bits of hope
like breadcrumbs
along the sidewalks
and silent porches
finding our way home
to our porch light
our beacon of belonging
summer will come
and winter will follow
footprints will fade
but not this indelible
wisp of memory

I'VE HAD MANY great meals, but I think the best meal I ever had—and perhaps ever will—was at the Café Baraka, a small store-front restaurant off Central Square in Cambridge, Massachusetts. It was my birthday.

Ginger had arranged for a group of our friends to help celebrate another successful year of aging on my part. Our ritual for most of our marriage has been for her to take me to eat some sort of ethnic food we have not yet tried. That year, it was North African food. My birthday falls in December, so the evening was cold as we wandered off of Mass. Ave., trying to find the place in a time before GPS devices and smartphones. We walked past it twice before our band of ten or twelve stumbled into our own little street-level Upper Room, which had enough space for us and that was about it. Tapestries and travel posters adorned the walls. Well-pillowed benches and chairs sat on each side of the long table that became our home for the evening. There was one server and, as best we could tell, one chef. The calligraphy on the walls spoke to their Muslim faith, so there was no wine that evening. We ordered Algerian lemonades and hot mint tea and then began to look at the menu, which offered one culinary adventure after another flavored with cumin, coriander, harissa, and orange blossom water.

We each ordered an appetizer and, as they began to arrive one at a time, we realized two things: the chef was working alone and we were in for a long and wonderful evening. In a way we could never have planned, each dish became an exercise in sharing and an expression of community. As a new plate arrived, each diner tasted it and then passed it on to the next friend along with some statement of what to expect from the dish. We moved from appetizers to entrees following the same pattern of tasting and sharing, and then ended the evening with the aromas of cardamom coffee and more mint tea swirling around and landing in the fertile field of our friendship and laughter. When we wandered back out into the winter night some five hours later, I had been given the gift not only of a meal but also of a marker. There was life as I knew it before the Baraka Café and life after it, as has become true of my birthday dinners from Algerian and Ethiopian to Mongolian, Turkish, and Afghani.

Communion is the same kind of mile marker. When Paul talks about the meal, leaning hard into what was an already established ritual, he said to use it as a chance to clear the air, to get things straight, to make room for what is to come, what needs to be born. We are called to create a before and an after. Any meal that holds a sense of ritual offers that chance for repentance and renewal, or the chance to both start and end something. The sacramental meal of bread and wine is even more charged with possibilities. Whom do I need to forgive? Of whom do I need to ask forgiveness? Who needs to know they are not alone? Whom can I bring to the Table? And there are other questions. What has happened since the last time we were here? What new dreams do I have? What has been lost? Who has gone? Who has arrived? What hunger needs to be fed?

Most of my Communions have been in congregationally structured denominations, which means we pass the plates of bread and the trays of small cups from person to person down each pew, deacons on either end to move the elements from row to row. The theological underpinnings for our actions were best expressed by Carlyle Marney, who said it was a way of reminding everyone at the Table that "your priest was at your elbow." In just a couple of motions, we were invited to both serve and be served, to be reminded we are part of the Great Banquet. That perspective is not lost on me, however, when I have occasion to share the meal by moving to the altar to be fed by the priest, or when I receive the elements by intinction. The sacred bread line, a better dressed version of the same leading into the local soup kitchen, is a sign of connectedness and solidarity. We want to take our turn to mark the day, to remember, as I learned as a Baptist, "who we are and Whose we are," to come hungry and to go away fed, and to be reminded once more we are not alone.

When Ginger and I celebrated our anniversary last year, we went to a fancier restaurant than usual because she was willing to accommodate my culinary adventuresomeness in the name of love. We chose a great place in our neighborhood called Piedmont, a name drawn from our region of North Carolina, which, in turn, borrowed it from the food and farm region of northern Italy. The restaurant is owned by a chef named Marco who also owns the farm where much of the food is grown and raised. The freshness requires the menu to change daily, which affords him and his staff the chance to add intensely personal touches. When they handed us our menus, "Happy Anniversary" was printed across the top of the page. I had told them about the occasion when I made the reservation and they took the time and effort to mark it. As we read down we noticed one of the appetizers was called "Ham and Eggs"—a playful description for a plate of deviled ham, deviled eggs, and homemade crostini. I'm a ham fan and Ginger loves deviled eggs, so we split the eight-dollar plate. What arrived at our table was a delicately crafted appetizer that held one hard-boiled egg that had been split and filled and placed on top of an ounce or two of deviled ham. The bread was stacked on the side. After the server had walked away, Ginger commented on the cost of the item relative to the size of the serving; then she tasted the egg.

"Wait," she said. "That's the best deviled egg I've ever had."

"That's because the eight dollars bought the chef some time," I answered. "The difference between good food and great food has to do with time."

What is true of cooking is also true of eating. The difference between a good meal and a great meal is time—how long we linger at the table—whether it be a special occasion or a Sunday supper of leftovers. To break our schedule as we break bread is an opening for the Spirit. A thin place. The Celtic idea of the thin places in life where the barriers between heaven and earth almost disappear is as ancient as it is well traveled. I don't remember how or when I first learned of it, but I do know food, for me, is one of life's quotidian thinners. One of the ways we draw nigh is breaking bread together, thus breaking down barriers and opening our hearts.

All I have to do is start to sauté garlic (which is the beginning of any number of dishes at our house) and Ginger will call from the other room, "What smells so good? I just love that smell." She loves it because it makes time stand straight up, stacking all the days and nights our kitchen has smelled that way, all the evenings we've walked through the North End of Boston, all the memories of how good it tastes to smear roasted garlic on crusty bread or how rich the olive oil tasted when we were together in Turkey tracing the steps of the Apostle Paul. Instead of reaching back from present to past, time stands on its head allowing our hearts to move fluidly through all the memories, letting us trace our steps and stack up the stones, revealing forgotten hopes and feelings, and making an indelible mark—an altar to which we can return. Good meals are not efficient. They take time. The thick skin of our hearts cannot grow thin in a matter of minutes. Memories cannot call us to confession, compassion, and forgiveness in an instant. "Be still and know that I am God," is the admonition. Breathe deep. Sit still. Chew slowly.

In the late eighties, my friend Billy Crockett and I were in the middle of writing songs he would later record. We had been writing songs together for several years in a collaboration born of community: the songs were born out of our friendship and out of my wanting new songs for my youth group to sing at camp. The record became *Any Starlight Night*, which was full of stories of people learning how to live with the pain and wonder that make up our existence. As we shaped the album, one of the subjects on our short list was a song about Communion.

Ken Hugghins and I have been friends since I met him in 1974 during my first semester at Baylor University, which was his senior year. He was a lean and wiry guy who could grow facial hair on command and sing like Gordon Lightfoot. We became close friends in seminary. He went to serve as minister to students at a church in Abilene, Texas, after several years working on college campuses. Our friendship held more than its share of late night discussions about love and life and sex and death, along with the theology that shoots through all of them. Our record collections provided the soundtrack. In one late night talk, he told me about a Communion experience with his students. As I remember, they were reading the account of the Last Supper in Matthew in which Jesus poured the wine and then said, "I will not drink of this cup until I drink it new with you in the Kingdom of my Father." As he finished reading, one of his students raised her glass and said, "Here's to the Day." The rest of the group returned the toast and then they all drank together. As he told me the story, I wrote down her words, and they became the title of our song.

Though we remember Jesus' death in the meal, it is not a wake. We are not gathering in quiet to share covered dishes brought by friends and share remembrances; there is more to the meal than the overtones of betrayal and despair that mark that night in the Upper Room. This side of the Resurrection, our deep memory calls us to profound expectation. We remember why we are eating and drinking together and who we are waiting to join us once again. We expect things to have changed since we last ate and anticipate more change to come. We dream out loud of a better world to come. I could see Ken's students in my mind's eye as I wrote:

> Pieces of life laid on the table
> Here is the blood poured out in love
> Fill this cup, raise it up
> Here's to the day, my friend
> Time draws a line down innocent faces
> Tears mark the dreams that never come home
> Fill this cup, raise it up
> Here's to the day that's coming

When I wrote those words, the Berlin Wall had yet to come tumbling down, Nelson Mandela was still in prison, Eastern Europe was still under Soviet control, and the crowds had only recently been dispersed in Tiananmen Square. Though the winds of change shook our hearts, we were aware of all that was not yet. The sense of the Day That Was Coming was not only about Jesus' words, but also about how we might incarnate our solidarity with those for whom darkness was the most present reality. The next verse says:

> Can you say it for the ones whose voices are silenced?
>
> Can you say it for the ones who've never been free?
>
> Can you fill this cup, raise it up—
>
> Here's to the day that's promised,
>
> God speed the day . . .

I can remember sitting in the spare room in Billy's house in Manchaca, Texas, staring at my pages of snippets and scribblings and wondering how the song would end. I thought about sitting with Reed at camp, about Mandela and Tutu and Martin Luther King Jr., the students with their glasses held high, the audacity of Billy and me thinking we could say something important about Communion, and how much I believed in what I was writing, when these words came:

> Gather in close now, cling to each other
>
> Sing to the night, you don't sing alone
>
> Fill this cup, raise it up
>
> Here's to the day—remember[11]

When the record came out, Billy received a request from someone to make a video of the song. He agreed, and a few weeks later, he greeted me holding a videotape when I arrived in Manchaca. The video consisted of one still photograph. As the piano introduction began, the camera moved slowly like a Ken Burns documentary across the faces of a group of people posed together in the middle

---

11 Billy Crockett and Milton Brasher-Cunningham (Radar Days Music and Walking Angel Records, 1990). Used by permission.

of a forest clearing. The picture was black and white. The faces were intent and determined. In the center of the group, one person held a loaf of bread wrapped in a white cloth and a chalice. They were sharing Communion in the middle of the woods in Romania, where it was illegal to worship. Their determination not to forsake their gathering together had led them deep into the forest. As I recall the picture, they were not smiling, yet there was no fear in their eyes. I could see hope. They went into the woods because they believed the day would come when they could eat together openly. As the words and music played underneath the image, I realized we had written more than we knew. There was a time before the song and a time after, a time before and after the photograph as well. Here's to the day.

In the summer of 2011, I was a part of an intentional gathering of believers in the forest of North Carolina for the inaugural Wild Goose Festival. The wild goose is a Celtic metaphor of the Holy Spirit. Though we gathered without fear of government reprisals, there were some who castigated the event for being too liberal or too unorthodox because of its commitment to inclusivity. We closed the festival with a Communion service. People circled in small groups all over the grassy field in front of the main stage and shared pieces of pita bread and wine from mason jars as our final statement of solidarity after four days of art and words and music.

My volunteer duties at the festival made me late to the service. I was standing under a tree watching the groups share their meal. One person in a circle not far from me noticed me standing there and invited the whole group to come and include me, which they did. When we finished, we began to hug and say, "I hope I see you again next year." Before and after. Here's to the day.

About a year after we moved to Durham, I was invited to join a group from our church for a Japanese dinner. Of the eight of us who gathered around the table, three had lived in Japan (one of them teaches Japanese at a local high school) and one had Japanese relatives. The point of the meal was to lean into those experiences and so we had an authentic Japanese meal: sukiyaki and nabe.

I've cooked a lot of different things, but I know very little about Japanese cooking other than I'm a big fan of the eel roll at our supermarket's sushi bar. When I got to the house where we were eating, people were in the kitchen chopping the vegetables that were going into the dinner: daikon, bok choy, napa cabbage, a variation on a scallion whose name I forget, and a couple of very cool kinds of mushrooms (enokitake and something translated as crab mushrooms). There were also some jelly-like noodles, cubed tofu, and thinly sliced beef.

At the meat-eating end of the table, where I was sitting, there was an electric skillet. The chief cook began by adding a little oil and then sautéing some of the meat. She added the daikon, the bok choy, and the cabbage to let them soften a bit and then began building the sauce, adding vegetable broth, soy sauce, sugar, and aji mirin. As we watched and talked, she added the rest of the ingredients and let them simmer in the sauce for a bit as she cooked the meal right in front of us. We then filled our bowls and ate until the skillet was empty and the room was full of stories. The meal gave those with first-hand experience of Japan the chance to talk of how the country had marked them, about their before and after.

On that same Saturday before Thanksgiving one year earlier, I finished my drive from Marshfield to Birmingham, my Cherokee packed with all the things that wouldn't fit in the PODS containers for our move to North Carolina. We spent the holiday at my in-laws and made the final leg of our journey the following week. Even though we were in a different location, I carried on my ritual of making the dinner. Thanksgiving is a marker for Ginger and me. It is a meal for which we gather in close, when the house fills up with people we love, and each one has a request for the dish that helps make the meal a thin place for them. My cornbread dressing recipe is one handed down in my family. For the first couple of years I cooked the dinner, I had to call my mother in the middle of everything because I couldn't find the recipe. What began out of necessity has become a part of the ritual of the meal. I call and ask for the recipe and make no real attempt to keep a copy anywhere in my notes. Truth is, after all these years, I know it by heart. Still, I look forward to the phone call.

A. W. Tozer wrote:

> Has it ever occurred to you that one hundred pianos all tuned to the same fork are automatically tuned to each other? They are of one accord by being tuned, not to each other, but to another standard to which each one must individually bow. So one hundred worshippers meeting together, each one looking away to Christ, are in heart nearer to each other than they could possibly be were they to become "unity" conscious and turn their eyes away from God to strive for closer fellowship. Social religion is perfected when private religion is purified.[12]

The Eucharist is that tuning fork for me, even though it mixes my metaphors, because it marks time: it makes a before and an after. I've been a part of churches in Africa and Texas and Massachusetts and now North Carolina and celebrated the Eucharist in all of them. Though the meal might not have been served in the same way, it was the same meal—the same meal shared by Christians across the centuries, to be shared for the centuries to come, each morsel of bread remembering who has gone and who has arrived, marking a new day with the gifts of God for the people of God, and reaffirming the promise of what is to come. Here's to the day.

---

12 A. W. Tozer, *The Pursuit of God* (Camp Hill, PA: Wing Spread Publishers, 2006), 90.

Cornbread Dressing

This is the recipe that has been handed down:

    4 cups broken cornbread

    1 onion, diced small

    1 cup celery, diced

    2 eggs, beaten

    1/2 cup melted butter

    salt and pepper

    4 cups boiling water (you won't use it all)

Put the broken cornbread in a bowl and add the onion, celery, butter, eggs, and salt and pepper. Slowly add boiling water, stirring as you go, until the mixture is wet, but not thin. Pour into a greased 9 x 9 pan and bake at 425 degrees for 30–40 minutes, or until it is set in the middle. (The original recipe doesn't have a time on it; depending on how much water you add and how dry you like it, you will have to decide when to take it out of the oven.)

Over the years, I have made a couple of changes: I cook five or six slices of bacon to crumble up in the dressing, and then I sauté the onion and celery in the bacon grease before adding them to the cornbread. I also season with Goya Adobo. Last, I use chicken stock instead of water for the liquid. Serves 8–10.

Striking Out

Congregation

God has made a habit of gathering
undesirables, the less than perfect,
or at least those as broken as they
are brazen—I could name names
but it serves just as well to look in
a mirror, or around most any room
filled with the fallen and faithful;
what privilege I enjoy I have not
earned; any hardship or suffering
I have endured was not inflicted;
what sense of belonging I have
known, what love I have found—
or has found me—came wrapped
in the dusty envelope of humanity,
fraught with fingerprints that point
to both a checkered past and a promise
that love binds us together because
it is not earned, but given and received.

THIS PAST SPRING I was a part of a group at my church that met to read Walter Brueggemann's book *The Bible Makes Sense*.[13] It has been my good fortune to be one of the teachers of the class, since the book is one I have read and reread over the years. Brueggemann, like Frederick Buechner and Madeleine L'Engle among others, is one of my "book friends" who have been faithful companions. At the end of one of the chapters Brueggemann asks the question, "How would God organize the world?" as a way to get us to think about how we can similarly organize our lives to reflect the imagination of our Creator. I smiled at the question because my particular way of organizing, whether it's my world or my desk, might best be described as free association or, more simply, chaos. It's not that I don't know where things are, it's just the coherence of the system is not apparent to anyone except me. My mind works much the same way: when I begin thinking about a particular idea, I pull things together across time and space; old stories become new again and find new life in connections.

When I think about how God organizes the world, I don't see straight lines and file cabinets. The "ring of fire" solar eclipse happened because the moon orbits the earth elliptically rather than symmetrically. I have learned in planting vegetables that corn has to be planted in squares rather than lines because of the way the plants pollenate. Weeds grow regardless of what I do. The layers and layers of stars speak to a God more prone to whimsy and extravagance than columns and charts, more interested in questions than answers, more determined to love than to judge. When I think

---

13 Walter Brueggemann, *The Bible Makes Sense* (Winona, MN: St. Mary's Press, 1977).

of how to talk about how God organizes the world, I find myself moving from Brueggemann to Buechner to Boston and baseball, the saddlebags of my mind stuffed with moments and memories, words and wisdom—all bread for the journey.

I was in college when I first discovered Buechner's *Wishful Thinking: A Theological ABC*. In the process of writing this chapter I felt something pulling from the recesses of my memory and I realized I was leaning into words he wrote long ago. Hand-me-downs are at the heart of our communal life of faith as we pass words and thoughts along in the same way we share The Meal. Once again, I am fed by what he said:

> It is make believe. You make believe that the one who breaks the bread and blesses the wine is not the plump parson who smells of Aqua Velva but Jesus of Nazareth. You make believe that the tasteless wafer and cheap port are his flesh and blood. You make believe that by swallowing them you are swallowing his life into your life and that there is nothing in earth and heaven more important for you to do than this.[14]

All by itself, "believe" isn't much of a verb when it comes to matters of faith. Our daily existence is a matter of life and death and requires a word with more heart and hope than one that merely "expresses confidence," according to the dictionary. Something happens when we say *make* believe, when we add a more active and demanding partner. Make: to bring into being, to create; make believe: to imagine. To say we believe in God is merely voicing our assent; to make believe—to imagine who God is and what God would do in and through us—is to let the Spirit wreak havoc with our hearts. We come to the Table to imagine what it feels like to forgive and be forgiven, to imagine how we live out our lives and faith together, to imagine how we can incarnate the love of Christ to the whole wide world. We make believe we can forgive one another.

---

14 Frederick Buechner, *Wishful Thinking: A Theological ABC* (San Francisco: HarperSanFrancisco, 1973), 63.

We make believe we can heal one another. We make believe it matters to be together in Christ—and it does.

If my father were organizing the world, it would be around sporting events. My brother and I were encouraged to play all the sports we could and to play them competitively because, as I recall my father saying in various fashions, someone had to win and it might as well be us. The only problem I had was I was an incredibly average athlete. Growing up in Africa, I was not exposed to all the organized sports that fill the schedule of American kids and I grew up playing soccer and cricket and softball in the backyard with the kids in the neighborhood, which meant I didn't have to be Number One. My one venture into school sports was at Nairobi International School when I was in ninth grade, and we had so few people we all had to be on the team, whether it was soccer or rugby or softball. When we returned to the States for good during my junior year in high school, I joined the choir and stayed on stage. I love sports as a fan, not an athlete, and I am a particular fan. I love baseball most of all because it is the sport most full of stories, the sport where the fans matter most, the sport that is about making errors and coming home. In a piece James Carroll wrote in the *Boston Globe* called "Baseball Communion," he said:

> The game means nothing, but while it's on, the game means everything. The game belongs to the players on the field, but their performance is insignificant unless beheld. Thus watching becomes, intermittently, the most intense of human acts. Famously a mere pastime, what lifts baseball out of the realm of triviality is the meaning the fans attribute to it. A ballpark's grandstands, therefore, matter as much as the lined field. The broadcast, too, becomes absolute, as entire populations pull up chairs.[15]

I read his words and I think of the great cloud of witnesses in Hebrews 12:1. Baseball is a great metaphor for how God would organize the world because failure is essential to both.

---

15 *The Boston Globe*, July 29, 2003.

I can better explain my attachment to failure, perhaps, by saying I am a lifelong fan of the Boston Red Sox. I was born in Texas, grew up in Africa, and have always pulled for the Sox, even when all I knew of them were the games we could get late at night on Armed Forces Radio. The Red Sox are my team. In 1967, I was in sixth grade and living in America for only the third year of my entire life. My parents were on leave from the mission field and we lived in Fort Worth where I walked each day to Hubbard Heights Elementary School, which was my first experience beyond kindergarten in an American school. Both my brother and I marveled at the kids in our class who had lived in the same house their entire lives. We were outsiders. As I tried to find my way into American life that fall, the Red Sox made an amazing late season run and won the pennant on the last day of the season. In those days television didn't control the sports schedule and there were afternoon games, even in the World Series. As I prepared to leave for school one morning, my dad said, "Would you like for me to write a note so you can come home and watch the Sox play this afternoon?" That moment defined my father in my mind. In later years, when I felt alienated from my family, his question reminded me I could not write him off. I don't remember what I said other than yes. I do remember walking home right after lunch and sitting on the couch with him as the Sox came back from being down to force a seventh game and raise our hopes they would win their first championship in fifty years, only to lose the game and the World Series, break my heart, and make me a fan forever.

Jesus spent a good deal of time talking about losing our lives, our pride, our place in line. He did little to climb the ladder to any sort of social or economic standing, choosing instead to surround himself with those who were accustomed to not being Number One. We share the Communion meal following his command to remember his death, which Frederick Buechner described as the "magnificent defeat," or, in parlance of my high school students, "epic fail." We come to the table to remember the failure, both his and ours, and to forgive and feed one another. This is how God organizes the world.

For ten of the years we were in New England, Ginger and I lived in an 1850 row house in the downtown neighborhood of Charlestown. Both the house and the neighborhood had survived a myriad of changes, but since the house was built two things had remained the same: it was located on a dead-end, one-way street, and it faced a park, which was deeded as a "mother's rest." The house had neither a front yard nor air conditioning, which meant that sitting at the open kitchen window was basically sitting on the sidewalk. One summer morning, I was sitting there drinking coffee with my friend Billy when a boy about seven or eight entered the park carrying a baseball bat. He had the whole place to himself. After wandering around a bit, he did what countless other boys had done. He picked up the bat, stepped up to an imaginary plate in a crowded imaginary ball park (Fenway, I assumed), and prepared to face whoever was pitching that particular afternoon. I looked up from my place in the stands in time to hear him swing and say, "Strike one." He stepped back, dusted off his tennis shoes, and stepped back into the batter's box. Another swing. "Strike two." This time we put down our coffee cups and became part of the scene, imagining it was the bottom of the ninth and everything was riding on the next pitch. We knew the script. He was going to hit it out of the park. We prepared to celebrate, even though he didn't know we were watching. He leaned in and slowly tilted the end of the bat back and forth above his head. Then the pitch. "Strike three," he said, and dropped the bat. His bat. His game. His pitcher. His imagination. And he struck out. Billy and I were both dumbfounded and, somehow, we understood. Failure is an organizing principle of our existence.

One of the reasons Billy was sitting in our house that morning was because we wrote songs together. One of my favorite songs we wrote was about Martin Luther King Jr., who remains one of our heroes because of his commitment to justice and love, to failure and faithfulness. "I may not get to the mountaintop," he said on the night before he was killed, even as he called people to never give up. The inspiration for our song about King came from a story about the captain of a cruise ship who deserted his ship when it began sinking in the Mediterranean. King represented the antithesis of the captain's lack of courage. The last two lines of the chorus read:

> sometimes you get to your bright tomorrow
>
> sometimes you've got to go down with the ship

Ginger and I had the privilege of standing on the balcony of the Lorraine Motel in Memphis where King was killed that Thursday in April 1968. The motel is now a civil rights museum and research center, even as we are still looking for the bright tomorrow.

In 2004, April 4 was a Communion Sunday at First Congregational Church in Hanover, where I was associate pastor. It was also opening day for the Red Sox, who were still the patron saints of hopeless baseball causes in those days. As we shared our joys and concerns during prayer time, Wally stood up with his hymnal open. He was a retired physician who made wooden bowls as a hobby. His spirit was as gentle as his hands. "I have a song for today," he said and then read these lines from Isaac Watts' great hymn, "O God, Our Help in Ages Past":

> Time, like an ever rolling stream bears all its
> sons away;
> they die, forgotten, as a dream dies at the
> opening day.[16]

Baseball is known as our national pastime: "an activity that makes time pass pleasantly." For those of us who are baseball fans, the first day of the season means marking time in innings rather than hours; in fly balls and strikeouts; in home runs and hot dogs. For those of us who are Red Sox fans—or Cubs fans, or Pirates fans, or pretty much anyone but a Yankees fan, it means choosing to dream in the face of impending defeat. As Terrence Mann said in *Field of Dreams*, "The one constant through all the years, Ray, has been baseball. America has rolled by like an army of steamrollers.

---

16 *The Psalms of David*, 1719.

It's been erased like a blackboard, rebuilt, and erased again. But baseball has marked the time."[17]

Baseball marks time in ways other sports do not because it is fundamentally about two things: making errors and coming home. When we come to the Table, we remember Jesus' death, which Frederick Buechner called "the magnificent defeat," and we offer one another fellowship and forgiveness.

When Wally stood up that Sunday, he had no idea we were beginning the season when the Sox would finally win a World Series, breaking an eighty-six-year drought. In the weeks that followed, Red Sox pennants and paraphernalia replaced graveside flowers in cemeteries all over New England. It didn't matter how many Octobers had come and gone since we had last won. As good as it felt, we also knew somehow that it wasn't going to become an every year thing. It was, after all, baseball. In 2006, we didn't even make the playoffs and life felt as though it was settling back to normal. In the middle of the summer of 2007, however, the Sox went on quite a tear and won five games straight. My friend Doug, who is an artist and one of the best receptacles of pure enthusiasm that I know, had a chance to go to Fenway in the middle of the streak along with two other friends, Jay and Marc. Daisuke Matsuzaka—our newest pitching sensation—was on the mound, the weather for the evening was picture perfect, a blue moon came up over the stands as darkness fell, and we lost. And it was all Doug's fault. Somewhere around the third or fourth inning, while we were still up 2–0, Doug told us the Sox lost every time he came to a game. Our whole section took it pretty well, until the sixth inning when the Indians scored six runs. Doug had gone down to get a beer as the Sox came to bat in the bottom of the inning and the first three batters hit singles. When he came back to his seat, the bases were loaded with no outs. Several of us in our section put on our "rally caps," turning them around or inside out, hoping something in our ridiculous appearance would foster a change in the situation. Things weren't going well so we resorted to magical

---

17 *Field of Dreams*, directed by Phil Alden Robinson, Universal Studios, 1989.

thinking to see if that would make a difference. "Are you sure you don't want to stay downstairs?" I asked. He sat down, the next three batters were retired, and we lost the game 8–4. We blamed Doug because we needed an explanation.

Our answer to failure, sometimes, is to assign blame or to choose guilt. Doug came back + we lost = Doug should be banned from Fenway. But bad things happen because life is difficult and painful even as it is full of joy and wonder. We strike out. We sin. We fail. And we come to the Table to find forgiveness and hope. As a child, I learned Hebrews 11:1 from the King James version: "Faith is the substance of things hoped for, the evidence of things not seen." Faith is trusting what I don't understand: that God is love and grace is true and I suffer. We all do. Making meaning of what we don't understand requires more than stepping over cracks, throwing salt over our shoulders, or sending money to televangelists. When it comes to nourishing our faith, guilt is nothing but empty calories. The substance of things hoped for lies in forgiveness and community; the evidence of things not seen is in the way we love one another. As Mumford and Sons sing in "Roll Away Your Stone,"

> it seems that all my bridges have been burned
>
> you tell me that's exactly how this grace thing works
>
> it's not the long walk home that will change this heart
>
> but the welcome I receive with every start[18]

In God's way of organizing the world, we are prodigals coming home every time we come to the Table. Faith, like baseball, is about making errors and coming home.

The modern game of baseball is a business as much as any other sport, which means players get cut and traded without much regard, sometimes, for the stories or the connections the fans have as they sit in the stands. In the middle of the 2004 season, the Red Sox traded Nomar Garciaparra right at the trading deadline in a move no one saw coming. He was one of our favorite guys, one of the

---

18 Mumford and Sons, "Roll Away Your Stone," from the album *Sigh No More* (Gentlemen of the Road / Island Records, 2009).

players who captured the spirit of the team, and then one day we woke up and he was no longer one of us. In the summer of 2010, in a week when the story of the Prodigal Son was the lectionary passage for the week, Nomar came back to Boston to retire, which was no easy feat. The terms under which he'd left were not good at all, and it was the October that followed—and perhaps, in part, because of the trade—that the Red Sox won the World Series for the first time in eighty-six years. Every time Nomar came back to Boston, regardless of the uniform he was wearing, the Fenway Faithful gave him a long standing ovation. Besides, he was the only player whose name, when said with a Boston accent, rhymed with homer, as in, "Come on, No-mah—hit a ho-mah." In 2010, spring training was in full swing and Nomar was not playing for anyone. He said he knew it was time to quit and he wanted to retire in a Red Sox uniform.

Then the Red Sox management did something that was more about people than profit, more about metaphor than money: they offered him a contract—a one-day, minor league contract—that allowed him to become a part of the organization once again. He signed the contract and then he was able to retire. At home. "The dream to play baseball in the big leagues started here," he said at his news conference. "I really wanted to have this be the last uniform I ever put on." The only thing missing was the meal.

In the King James version of the story in Luke, it says the Prodigal Son "came to himself" as he was feeding the pigs and realized it was time to go home for good. He realized he was prodigal, as in wastefully extravagant, and he had used himself all up, along with his possessions. The dictionary offers a second definition for prodigal: "giving in abundance; lavish or profuse," so we might also use the same adjective for the father who welcomed his son home with extravagant forgiveness and a barbecue to boot. They shared a propensity for extravagance; the father, however, knew how to spend himself in love.

Yes, I'm a Sox fan and I know I might be stretching the story a bit here, still I'm willing to stretch because one of ours that got lost came home. He was humble enough to ask and the Red Sox owner-ship was generous enough to find a way to make it work. Whatever happened between 2004 and 2010 was what happened, but the real story was he came home. And my guess is it was no different at the Prodigal Household in the parable. As they bit into the brisket, they told stories, too, of how the boy had run away, and how the father had pined at the front door day after day. "And then you came home," someone said. And they laughed and cried and told the story again, talking, I'm sure, with their mouths full.

Togetherness is not a myth, nor is it a given. In Jesus' parable of the Great Banquet (one of my personal favorites), the king told the servants to go out and compel people to come in until the hall was filled. When the disciples questioned if the five loaves and two fishes would be enough to feed everyone, Jesus told them to just start feeding people and trust they would have enough. The way I've always imagined the scene is, as the boy's lunch was passed and the unabashed sharing became obvious, others who had food of their own thought, "Well, I could share my lunch," and the next thing they knew they had leftovers. When we make believe we are in this together and that we are defined by both our failures and our forgiveness, we find room at the table and enough to feed everyone.

Josh Hamilton, who plays for the Texas Rangers, is having an exceptional year by all accounts. His batting average, as I write, is .389, which is enough to win the batting title, should he keep it up. Off the field, he is a man already acquainted with both failure and forgiveness. He is a recovering addict. The team has made a com-mitment to help him in his sobriety, even to the point of show-ering each other with nonalcoholic champagne when they won the American League Pennant. They made believe his addiction would not be the whole story, and he is writing quite a chapter this year. Yet, even as well as he is doing right now, he doesn't get a hit almost two out of every three times he comes to bat. In fact, most players are lucky to get a hit one out of four times at the plate. That's not the way baseball teaches us to interpret the stats, however. They talk about what he's accomplished, not how often he fails. Such is our chance when we come to the Eucharist. We have a chance to both take our failure seriously and reframe the story. Paul understood when he wrote in Romans, "More than that, we rejoice in our sufferings, knowing that suffering produces endurance, and endurance produces character, and character produces hope." Not hope in the sense of "I hope I do better next time," but hope as informed confidence in our Creator for whom failure is never the last word. God is personally acquainted with failure—as strange as that may sound—because of God's relationship with us. From wondering why Adam and Eve didn't show up for their evening walk in the garden, to seeing Abel's blood in the dirt, to telling Noah to build the Ark, to the people wandering in the wilderness, to Peter's denials and Judas' betrayal, all the way down to some things we'd prefer not to share, God is acquainted with grief, with failure. If that were not true, the hope we've been promised could not hold the weight of the world. In God's way of organizing, redemption requires a Redeemer who abides on both sides of the equation.

To know God knows what failure feels like strengthens my faith because I'm reminded that what lies beyond failure is love rather than success. We are always going to strike out more times than we hit it out of the yard, therefore we need each other to tell the stories and remember we are not alone. James Carroll says, "The game affirms the normalcy of physical communication with another—and with many others. That communion, we understand from an early age, is what we live for." Therefore, we step up to the plate, if you will, to break the bread and share the cup, remembering how God organizes the world: Jesus' magnificent defeat, our own spectacular failures, and the grace that saves us all.

Barbecue Bonfire Packs

This is a recipe that grew out of necessity. We had a dinner at the Hanover church to say thanks to the folks who had given money for our mission trip. We had a small crew to fix dinner for about fifty people. I kept trying to think of something that we could do that would be easy to cook and clean up. Here's what I came up with.

Cut 18-inch aluminum foil in two-foot pieces, one for each person.

Put a piece down and spray with non-stick spray. Then layer

10 Tater Tots (I needed some sort of precooked potato and Tots are the best.)

3 slices of zucchini (sliced about 1/4 inch at an angle)

half a piece of andouille sausage

1 boneless chicken thigh

barbeque sauce

1 onion slice

Close pack tightly and place on a baking sheet in a 350-degree oven for about 35 minutes. Before you serve it, open the pack and sprinkle with shredded cheese.

Comfort Food

similies

it's like the sand of life leaks
out from a hole in the sack
scattered then stomped
into the surface
but nothing gets lighter
the gravity of absence
crushes out the colors and
somehow grey weighs more
the shadows know things
they are not telling
now I see through a glass
darkly yes darkly
it's like death has an echo
that bounces off shadows
reverberates in emptiness
and makes love hurt
it's like that

I'VE LIVED IN Africa, Texas, New England, and North Carolina and found one thing in particular they all have in common: when someone dies, you bring food. Whether it's the wake or the evening after the funeral, people show up with covered dishes, casseroles, macaroni and cheese, pies and cakes, and anything else that would offer a tangible way of expressing solidarity and sympathy. As the evening wears on, family and friends of both the dead and the living eat, drink, and remember. And it matters that it's over a meal. My first acupuncturist, Jake, taught me that one of the key ideas in Chinese medicine is that digestion has to do with all that we take in. We digest everything from ideas to allergens, words to waffles, frittatas to fear. Our digestive system doesn't differentiate between the physical and the spiritual. Everything matters.

On the night he was to be betrayed, Jesus gathered with his disciples for their Passover meal. They had not, to that point, digested his warnings about what was about to come down. For Jesus, who could see the gathering storm, it was one last chance to tighten the bonds between them, so he brought them a meal they knew, a meal that had been digested over centuries, one that was as familiar and rich as it was basic. He took the bread and he broke it, giving it new meaning, giving them more to take in. He offered them the opportunity to understand more as time went by and they shared the bread again and again.

In my three years at the Hanover church, I learned that one of the strengths of that congregation was a group of women who could make a formidable amount of food appear at what seemed to be a moment's notice in the face of most any crisis. Part of their charge was to provide for collations, as they call them in New England, which are the meals after the funeral services. Each woman on the team had a particular dish she was known for and was expected to provide. The menu was fairly set and it was excellent. The sameness was not because they saw their jobs as perfunctory. They brought their best work. The ritual of the meal mattered. We, the church members, knew those dishes as funeral food: the physical stuff we digested as we took in the reality of the death of one of our loved ones. Each event was linked in the chain of time to those that had preceded it such that as we took it in again, we also took in the memory of those who had gone on before and we digested the new meaning of what it meant to be one of those left living.

"The art of losing isn't hard to master," Elizabeth Bishop writes in her poem "One Art,"[19] which describes the string of sorrows that make up our lives. As we grow and age, the task of learning how to be one of those left living becomes more and more essential. How do we digest our losses? How do we feed one another and provide the physical and spiritual nutrition we all need to survive? When we come to Communion, we do stand in the unbroken line of all who have come before us and those who will come after us, but unbroken only in the sense of continuous. None of us is unbroken by life. We come to re-member ourselves, to allow the Spirit of God to put us back together again as the Body of Christ, and by sharing the meal, we affirm we are all essential to that unity and connect-edness. Everybody matters, even though, in the course of history, most of our names will be known to only a few folks on either side of us before we become part of the great cloud of witnesses.

When I was a youth minister, I used a vase of water to demon-strate our fleeting presence on the planet. I would place my hand down in the water and say, "While my hand is in the water, you can see its place." Then I would pull my hand out of the vase; the water didn't leave a hole where my hand had been. "Can you find where my hand was?" I would ask. "The only evidence I have that my hand was there is that it's wet." I've spent my life saying goodbye

---

19 *The Complete Poems of Elizabeth Bishop* (New York: Farrar, Straus & Giroux, 1979).

and have yet to experience a time when it was easy to do, whether it was because of a move or a death. Losses are always difficult to digest. When we are together at the eucharistic Table, we can lean into the love that reminds us that goodbye, though essential vocabulary for those of us left living, is not an ultimate word.

We come to the Table to feed one another, to be fed and forgiven, and to try and find a fresh perspective, which means coming to terms with what Sting describes so beautifully in his song, "Fragile":

> on and on the rain will fall
> like tears from a star
> like tears from a star
> on and on the rain will say
> how fragile we are
> how fragile we are[20]

At the center of that vulnerability, we gather around the table to move through the pain and the uncertainty that life holds, to feed one another in Jesus' name. "Faith is taking the first step even when you don't see the whole staircase," Dr. King said. He was one who knew of both faith and fragility, and who knew what a circle of friends committed to God and to one another could do. Sometimes it is nothing more than coming together to eat and to pray.

"Love doesn't mean doing extraordinary or heroic things. It means knowing how to do ordinary things with tenderness," says Jean Vanier in *Living Gently in a Violent World: The Prophetic Witness of Weakness*. "Community is made of the gentle concern that people show each other every day. It is made up of the small gestures, of services and sacrifices which say 'I love you' and 'I am happy to be with you.' It is letting the other go in front of you, not trying to prove you are right in a discussion; it is taking the small burdens from one another."[21] It is deciding that every gesture we make, from passing the bread to passing one another in the hall, will be one that says, "We are in this together." We are the ones still living.

---

20 Sting, "Fragile," from the album . . . *Nothing Like the Sun* (A&M Records, 1987).
21 Stanley Hauerwas and Jean Vanier, *Living Gently in a Violent World: The Prophetic Witness of Weakness* (Downers Grove, IL: InterVarsity Press, 2008), 78.

During our time in Durham, I have been asked to dig one grave. It was a first for me. The call came early one morning from church friends saying their beloved beagle, Violet, was going to be put to sleep. Ginger was up and out of the house in minutes. About a half hour later she called and asked me to meet her at their house to bury their pet. I put my shovel in the back of my Cherokee and drove over to share in what was a very sacred time. They brought Violet down from the house, beautifully swaddled in a sheet, and laid her in the place we had dug at the bottom of the yard, next to the fence that backs up on the wooded land behind them. Nellie, their beagle puppy, ran around us as I dug, and they grieved, a visible sign of hope beyond the loss. As we were putting the grass back on top of the grave, Robin threw a piece of a root over the fence into the woods and said, "It's good to be on the edge of the wilderness."

Yes, and meaningful.

The physical act of digging the grave and placing the body of the dear little dog down in the dirt had a visceral effect on me. There was a time when people were more accustomed to living with death, and dealing with it. The old row houses in Boston have "coffin corners"—small indentions in the wall of the stairway so the coffin could make the turns when the body was brought into the house for the wake. People dug graves together, waked the body together, buried their loved ones and threw dirt on the coffin together. They got to say goodbye with body, mind, and heart in a way we do not these days. Our funeral rituals are quiet and solemn and do their best to keep us from seeing anything but flowers. I felt honored to get to share so practically and poignantly in the grief of our friends. It is good to be on the edge of the wilderness—together.

Making comfort food for friends in grief brings the same kind of physicality to compassion I found in working the shovel to make a place for Violet. Here is how we show our love, our solidarity: here is food my family has made for years; we are the ones who are here; let's eat.

My strawberry shortcake recipe is four generations old. Ma—my paternal great-grandmother who died shortly after I was born—gave the recipe to my mother. The recipe was a list of ingredients. Ma cooked by approximation and intuition, the same way I learned to cook in restaurants. My mother had to figure out the specific measurements so my father would be able to recognize the comfort food of his childhood. Since I have become a bit of a gardener, I've come to enjoy adding a savory touch to the sweet things I cook, so I took what was handed down to me and have begun to chop up some fresh basil into the shortcakes, which are pretty much sweet biscuits—a handful of basil, I guess; I don't really measure how much. I cut up the strawberries and toss them in a little sugar, make some fresh whipped cream with a touch of cinnamon, halve the biscuits, and make layers: biscuit, strawberries, whipped cream, biscuit, berries, cream. Each bite is full of both history and imagination, of family in both past and present tense.

Comfort food. Sometimes it's in the recipe, sometimes it's in the history, sometimes it's the place or the people around the table that carry the comfort, but we all have certain foods that evoke warmth and belonging. Mine range from Jack-in-the-Box tacos (yeah, the cheap ones) to my mom's strawberry shortcake to the Boston cream pie at Mike's Pastry in Boston's North End. And Communion.

When Jesus first broke the bread and served the wine around the table, he wasn't thinking in gourmet terms. He picked the most basic elements of their diet, the stuff they ate and drank every day. Even more, I think he simply made use of what was in front of him. As intentional as the meal was, I've never thought of it as rehearsed. The tension was building. Their little band was about to be broken up. He knew he was down to his last few words and he took the bread and broke it—perhaps tore open would be a better choice of verb—and handed out the pieces to his friends who had little idea of all that was coming unhinged all around them.

"Whenever you eat this meal, remember," he said.

Not remember as in don't forget, but re-member as in put back together again. When we gather together at the table whether in the Upper Room or any evening meal, sharing food is an act of solidarity, a chance to find and share comfort. Life, whether in Palestine or Pittsburgh, is a dismembering proposition. It tears us apart. As Buddha began his teachings, "Life is difficult." Classic understatement. What puts the comfort in food is the chance to re-member one another, to put ourselves back together, to see our place in the big picture, to find in the midst of the free fall of our existence the truth of God's indefatigable tether of grace that holds us and holds on.

It's the scene from *Ratatouille* when the cynical food critic tastes the movie's title dish and reconnects with the lost boy inside who loved savoring his mother's cooking more than criticizing it. And it's the closing scene from *Big Night* in which the two brothers find forgiveness over breakfast on the morning after their grandest failure. It is the family recipe handed down, the holiday gathering relived with the same dishes year after year, and it is the small taste-less wafers or morsel of bread and the small sip of wine that culmi-nates our worship together.

"Re-member," Jesus said. Remember me. Remember you. Remember us. "Everybody hurts," sings Michael Stipe of R.E.M., "find comfort in your friends." Comfort and safety are not the same thing. Nancy Wingo was a missionary in Lebanon for many years. She was speaking at a church in Texas before returning to Beirut at a time when Lebanon was the crisis point in the Middle East. After she finished speaking, a well-intentioned woman came up to her and said, "I will pray for your safety."

"Oh, no," Nancy said. "Please don't. If your prayers were answered, I wouldn't be able to go back because it is not safe. Pray that I will be faithful." Safety seeks to create a buffer. Comfort is better informed, more resilient, more valuable and vulnerable, more faithful. Bike helmets and seat belts only go so far; comfort gets into our bones and our taste buds. Comfort gives us the strength to carry on in the face of fear and grief and whatever else happens in the course of our days. We are the ones left living. May we feed one another well.

Strawberry Shortcake

Let's start with the cream.

>1 pint heavy whipping cream
>1/4 cup chopped basil
>1/4 teaspoon cinnamon

Mix the ingredients and heat in a saucepan on medium heat until it begins to simmer; don't bring it to a boil. Let it steep until it is cool enough to touch and then transfer to a bowl and put in the refrigerator until it is cold. (It won't whip unless it's really cold). When you are ready to whip it, strain the liquid, put it in a mixer, add sugar and vanilla to taste and let it whip.

Note: heat the cream before you begin everything else; whip it just before serving.

And now the strawberries.

>1 pint strawberries, hulled and sliced
>1/4 cup balsamic vinegar
>1/4 cup sugar
>2 tablespoons orange or lemon juice

The process, called macerating the strawberries, is simple, though the word sounds far more violent than the process deserves. Again, create this mixture ahead of time so the strawberries have time to do their thing in the sugar and vinegar, and keep it refrigerated until you are ready to serve.

Finally, the shortcakes.

> 2 cups flour
> 4 teaspoons baking powder
> 1/2 teaspoon salt
> 4 tablespoons sugar

Combine the dry ingredients and then cut in

> 1/2 cup butter (my great-grandmother used Crisco,
>   I'm sure)

I use my food processor. When crumbly, add

> 3/4 cup milk.

Mix until combined. Pour dough out on a floured surface and roll out just enough to make it about a half an inch thick. Cut into 4-inch rounds (I use a biscuit cutter) and place on an ungreased baking sheet. Bake at 450 degrees for 12–15 minutes.

To serve, cut the shortcake in half. Put a small dollop of whipped cream on the plate; turn the top of the shortcake over and place on the whipped cream. Add more cream, strawberries, the other half of the shortcake (also inverted), and then more cream and berries. Serves 8.

Defining Moment

sunday sonnet #3

I had a church-less weekend since Sunday was my turn
 to stay at home with Reuben, who is ailing;
 I planted in the garden and gave the beds a turn
 While he sat and snored and set the "z"'s a-sailing.
 I was not there to stand in line to taste the Bread
  and Cup,
 the food that's fed the faithful across time;
 but today I shared a meal with friends we'd
  gathered up,
 and found our supper sacred and sublime.
 "Remember me as often as you do this," we
  repeat
 in our ritual of worship and redemption;
 but the Body is re-membered most every time we
  eat
 when we share the meal with focus and intention.
 After sharing food with friends, there is this that
  must be said:
 'tis no surprise they recognized him in the
  breaking of the bread.

S ERMONS GROW OUT of conversations at our house. Sometime early in the week, Ginger will begin talking about the upcoming lectionary passage, or I will ask what she is preaching on, and then we play "add-on" as the week progresses. In the meantime, of course, she is reading and studying and praying her way through her preparation; I just chime in from time to time. The process reflects the way we deal with most things in our marriage, bouncing them back and forth like rocks in a tumbler to see what we can polish up together. She was working on a sermon recently based on Psalm 23 and Jesus' description of himself as the Good Shepherd in John 10. The most persistent memory I have attached to the metaphor comes from my father's preaching when I was a teenager. As I recall, it was about the time Phillip Keller wrote *A Shepherd Looks at Psalm 23*, which was a thoughtful and helpful book even though it romanticized the relationship between the shepherd and the sheep.

"When Jesus called us sheep it wasn't a compliment," my father would say in a tone glazed in sarcasm. "Sheep are the dumbest animals. All they know how to do is follow. If one does something stupid, they all do it." In Southern terms, Jesus calling us sheep is the messianic equivalent of someone tilting her head to the side ever so slightly and saying, "Well, bless your heart." I told the story to Ginger one afternoon and a couple of days later she came back with an alternate take on the herd mentality my father deemed so worthy of mocking. The instinct to herd is not necessarily a sign of stupidity. Rather than see it as reason for derision, what if we looked at it as an intrinsic drive toward togetherness? Yes, if one sheep goes off a cliff, the others will follow. The shepherd, then, calls them away from the cliff and towards another expression of their community. Jesus talks about sheep again in Matthew 25:35–36 and compliments them: "for I was hungry and you gave me food, I was thirsty and you gave me something to drink, I was a stranger and you welcomed me, I was naked and you gave me clothing, I was sick and you took care of me, I was in prison and you visited me"—together.

We have various words to define how we gather together: group, mob, herd, gang, throng, crowd, audience, congregation. We have gathered to destroy neighborhoods, to burn crosses, to march for freedom, to protest wars, to demand justice, to raise money, to get new smartphones, and to share Communion. When we come to the table, we come together. My friend Bob Bennett wrote one of my favorite songs about the Eucharist, "Jesus in Our Time."

> Countless legions of the faithful
> Crossing every generation
> Hand-to-shoulder in an unbroken line
> Lead us to this Sabbath morning
> We humbly count ourselves among them
> To seek and find the face of Jesus
> In our time
> Though an imperfect congregation
> Full of folly and of doubt
> We presume to ask our questions
> Then we wrestle with their finding out
> We break the bread and pass the cup
> And try to bear each other up
> To live the mystery
> Of Jesus in our time
> There are those who are among us
> Who believe they are not worthy

We offer you the Word of Life
We bid you come and dine
Upon the mercy we have tasted
And the love given so freely
Come take your place at table now
With Jesus in our time
And as He promised
So we proclaim
He will be among us
As we gather in His name
To heal the broken-hearted
To ease our troubled minds
We want to know You
To follow You
Jesus in our time[22]

Earlier in the book, I made the distinction between habit and ritual, between doing things because they become familiar and meaningful repetition. Communion is a ritual act: we do it again and again because we mean to do so. I want to make another semantic distinction, this time between rule and commandment. I see a rule as something you follow in order that you don't get punished. When we break rules there are consequences. For many of us, then, we follow the rules to avoid the consequences. Not necessarily a bad motivation, but it only goes so far. Jesus talked about commandments: love God with everything that you are and love your neighbor as yourself. A commandment is like a rule in that we are expected to follow it. The difference is what lies beneath. A commandment is a call to a larger look, to a wider view, to a creative response. We follow the commandments in order that we might grow to become more of who God calls us to be and in order that we might be more unified. Commandments hold more than a

---

22 Bob Bennett, "Jesus in Our Time," from the album *Small Graces* (Bright Avenue Songs [ASCAP], 1996), www.bobbennett.com. Used by permission.

cause-and-effect equation. To follow Christ's commandments is to set the contagion of grace in motion in our time. In our time.

One of my father's favorite Bible stories is the story of Esther. I can remember him summarizing the story with energy and wit as he talked about how King Ahasuerus saw Esther's beauty and made her queen, even though she was Hebrew and her people were his slaves in exile; how Mordecai, her uncle and a Hebrew priest, told her not to give away her true identity until the right moment; how Haman planned a mass execution of Hebrews who would not capitulate to his rules; and how, at the climactic moment, Mordecai told Esther it was time to act with these words: "And who knows whether you have not come to the kingdom for such a time as this?"(4:14, ESV). My dad's eyes would glisten with a mixture of tears and resolve as he applied those words to my brother and me and called us to see the time is now. I love Mordecai's call to his niece and have spent many years wondering when my time would come, when it would be my moment. I've seen those kinds of moments in the lives of others like Martin Luther King Jr. or Bishop Oscar Romero, and read about others, but I have not had a moment in my life where I was aware that history hung in the balance. Until now. And that moment is in coming to understand that coming to the Table together defines us. Who knows that we are in this world for such a time as this: to offer food and drink to one another, to become the Body of Christ, the incarnation of God's love and grace in our world, to keep the commandments to love God and self and one another, to be changed by the presence of Christ in us.

Take. Eat. And remember. Durham CAN (Durham Congregations, Associations, and Neighborhoods) is a community organizing group made up of a wide cross-section of people from across our city who connect to bring about necessary change. They have organized neighborhood audits, for example, when people walked the streets of various neighborhoods—particularly some of the poorer ones—and made note of all the things that needed to be fixed, giving the information to the city. But that's not all. Then they invited the city manager, who stood before their assembly while one of the Durham CAN leaders asked him if he would be accountable to come back in ninety days and report on how the needs on the list were being addressed. The manager said he would, and he did. They didn't simply collect the information and pass it along; they worked to create a defining moment for everyone involved. Durham CAN doesn't raise money or hire lobbyists. They connect people in the community and bank on the relationships to call people to accountability. The trust of the organization is in the power of relationships. At one meeting, Ginger introduced me to Mauricio, whom she had met at an earlier gathering. He had been the English-to-Spanish translator for the meeting since about half the crowd were native Spanish speakers. He was a small man with a huge voice, and both his eyes and his speech sang with joy.

Mauricio is from El Salvador and came to the U.S. in early 1980 at the encouragement of his mentor, Bishop Oscar Romero, who helped him and several other young Salvadorian men get out of the country to tell El Salvador's story and to escape being killed by the death squads. Romero himself was assassinated in March of the same year. I was speechless. I was standing next to someone in Durham, North Carolina, who was standing next to me because of the actions of one of the heroes of my faith. For a moment, I stood in a small church connected across miles and years to someone who had helped to shape my faith, connected hand to hand, person to person.

The incidental contact of an introduction, a conversation, or the passing of the bread and cup are the stuff of glory, of community, of incarnation. We make our ways across oceans and opinions, across aisles and attitudes in small steps and gentle gestures much more often than in huge leaps and great actions. We serve one another, hand to hand, all the way back to the Upper Room. We are defined, redeemed, and recognized in the breaking of the bread. Every time we eat, we articulate who we are and to whom we belong. We are called to be God's people, the church. Though I can speak of God's call, I can't say I have ever heard God speak out loud. Whatever

God's voice actually sounds like, I think I come close to hearing it when our children lead worship. One Sunday, they led our call to worship by lining up in front of the Communion table and singing with holy gusto:

> I am the church, you are the church
> we are the church together
> all who follow Jesus all around the world
> we are the church together
> the church is not a building
> the church is not a steeple,
> the church is not a resting place
> the church is a people
> we're many kinds of people
> with many kinds of faces
> all colors and all ages
> from all times and places
> and when the people gather
> there's singing and there's praying
> there's laughing and there's crying
> sometimes, all of it saying
> I am the church, you are the church
> we are the church together
> all who follow Jesus all around the world
> we are the church together[23]

Their singing was evidence of the Incarnation, shown in the abandon with which they inhabited the words they sang and the tenacity of their hand gestures; they weren't fooling around. As they called us to worship, they called us to incarnate our faith not only as we passed the Bread and the Cup, but also as we passed the Peace during the service and as we passed the snacks at Coffee Hour. As

---

23 Hymn #109, "I Am the Church," from *My Heart Sings Out*, ed. Fiona Vidal-White (New York: Church Publishing Inc., 2005).

Augustine said, "You are the body of Christ and its members. . . . It is your own mystery that is placed on the Lord's table. And it is to what you are that you reply."[24] "The Word became flesh," John says at the beginning of his gospel (1:14). Paul's use of the body of Christ as the metaphor for the church suggests the Word stayed flesh. Mary Oliver says, "The Spirit likes to dress up like this: ten fingers, ten toes, shoulders, and all the rest."[25] We are the Church, the Body, the Word still made flesh: Love with skin on. Together, that is.

I love the line in the song that says, "The church is not a resting place." I remember my father telling a story years ago of a person leaving church one Sunday morning and telling him they would not be back. "I don't come to church to be made uncomfortable," they said. If we are the church, then we are not only Love with skin on, but also Pain and Grief and Hope and Joy and Despair incarnate. We are people deciding to be together, which means to be both comforted and uncomforted. It means we ought to be looking at one another and at our world with the same holy gusto with which our children sang.

I'm not sure where in my theological education—maybe Sunday school—I learned there were different ways of understanding what happens to the bread and the cup when we eat and drink the eucharistic meal. There were, of course, the stained glass words leaded with centuries of explanation: transubstantiation, consubstantiation. There were also the variations on the continuum from it actually becoming the physical body and blood of Christ to the elements being "nothing more" than symbols of God's love, which was the Baptist explanation I was given. My training as an English major taught me that saying, "nothing more than a symbol" missed the point and the power of symbolism, regardless of the other explanations, because a symbol always stands for something important, something with meaning, something for us to digest.

My training as a chef and my understanding of nutrition have

---

24 Augustine of Hippo, Sermon 272, *The Eucharist*, trans. Daniel Sheerin (Wilmington, 1986), 95.
25 "Poem," from *Dream Work* (New York: Atlantic Monthly Press, 1986).

taught me that what we eat becomes something else, once digested. My mother-in-law and I have an ongoing discussion about fat in which she has yet to trust me when I tell her the fat we eat doesn't turn into fat in our bodies. The sugar, however, is a different story.

Food becomes energy, sustenance, fat, and fuel for our existence. Food infused with meaning—the ritual food of the collation, for example—becomes more than physical. It becomes memory, comfort, love, and even hope. My great-grandmother's shortcake recipe becomes an ancestral connection to a woman I met when I was too young to remember in a family that has done little to husband the family tree. That recipe is my genealogy.

As disciples of Jesus Christ, we are called to struggle against everything that leads us away from the love of God and neighbor. Repentance, fasting, prayer, study, and works of love help us return to that love. We are invited, therefore, to commit ourselves to love God and neighbor by confessing our sin and by asking God for strength to persevere in our disciplines. We are called to struggle against everything that leads us away from love—from life together. We are called to work with intentionality toward everything that galvanizes us, that tightens the ties that bind, that reminds us life is a team sport, not an individual event.

One of the prayers of confession to which I continue to return is in *The Book of Common Prayer*. I go back there because of the particular phrase that asks forgiveness for "the things we have done and the things we have left undone."[26] In the call to do all we can to love one another and live together, often our omissions are those things that cause the cracks to appear, allowing us to drift apart without realizing what we have set in motion. Yes, we can and do inflict damage by what we do and say, still it seems what gets left undone soon becomes forgotten and paved over by life's other demands, burying necessary relationships like ancient cities under the dust and layers of modern life. Christine Lavin has an old song

---

26 The Book of Common Prayer (New York: Church Hymnal Corp., 1979), 360.

called "The Moment Slipped Away"[27] in which she describes missed opportunities and things left undone—small, significant chances—leaving both her and the person unencountered lost in the wake of what might have been. In gestures both small and large, what we leave undone opens a gap that gets filled with something other than love. Consistent, intentional, determined, tenacious love that leaves no stone unturned puts the solid back in solidarity.

Jesus knelt among the gnarly olive trees in the Garden of Gethsemane to pray just before he was arrested for the last time, and he prayed, "Make them one." Not keep them safe or let them win or make them rich and powerful. Make them one. He knew what we all learn rather quickly as we grow up: the forces of life are fragmenting. We are pushed apart and pulled away from each other. We learn to blame and to betray. We learn to look out for Number One. We learn we can't take care of everyone, so we have to take care of ourselves. Not long before he prayed, Jesus sat with his disciples around the table and, as he served them bread, he said, "Every time you do this, remember me." What if we could hear those words as an invitation to communion and community in every meal, in every cup of coffee, in every beer at the pub: every time you eat and drink, look each other in the eye and remember me, remember the love that binds you and do whatever you have to do to forget the lies you have learned that tear you apart.

The point of life is not to be right, or safe, or famous, comfortable, or rich, or powerful. None of those is a sign of success or God's favor or significance, particularly when our power and wealth and safety require someone else to be poor and weak and scared. The point of life is to be together. To love one another—all the one anothers—and to struggle against everything that leads us away from that love.

---

27 Christine Lavin, "The Moment Slipped Away," from the album *Beau Woes and Other Problems of Modern Life* (Rounder Records, 1987).

White Chocolate, Cranberry, and Pumpkin Seed Cookies

Preheat oven to 350 degrees.

3 cups flour

3/4 teaspoon baking powder

3/4 teaspoon salt

Mix dry ingredients together and set aside.

1 cup (2 sticks) butter, at room temperature

1 cup packed brown sugar

1 1/2 cups white sugar

2 eggs, at room temperature

1 1/2 teaspoons vanilla

Cream butter in electric mixer and then add sugars and mix until fluffy. Take your time: let the mixer run a good 6–8 minutes. Add the eggs one at a time, mixing well. Add vanilla. Add the flour mixture gradually, mixing until just combined. Then add

1 package (11 ounces) white chocolate chips

1 cup dried cranberries

1 cup roasted, salted pumpkin seeds

Mix just until the added ingredients are well distributed throughout the dough. Drop on an ungreased cookie sheet and bake for 11–13 minutes. Makes about four dozen cookies.

Afterword:
What the Food Becomes

dinner time

at the end of the day
when the day's had its way
and we sit at the table together
there is something profound
in being gathered around
to give thanks for both table and tether
bring your joy and your pain
and let's gather again
our sustenance lies in our sharing
yes the rite of our meals
makes a thin place that's real
and grows bonds quite resistant to tearing

B ROTHERS AND SISTERS, *from where have you come?* Such was the question that greeted us as we prepared to share Communion on Maundy Thursday. Those of us scattered across the sanctuary had come from different places. The answer we were called to give in unison was compelling:

We have come from the dust, and from the earth, and from the breath of God.

I had spent the afternoon before the service digging in the dirt, planting azaleas and hydrangeas and camellias and gardenias and all the other things that ought to grace the front yard of a Southern home. As I sat in the pew, I looked down at my hands to see the dirt still under my fingernails. Something about digging in the dirt centers me, encourages me—and it appears to be at an existential and theological level: I am handling the very building blocks of my existence. The difference between me and the topsoil is breath. God's breath. As we sat in the pew, I could feel the air in my own lungs and hear my breathing, as well as the breaths around me.

And why have you come?

None of us was there for the same reason, or so I assumed. I was one of the readers in the Tenebrae service; I was also there because I love this service as much as any during the year. And, again, we were called to answer in unison:

We have come to receive the bread and the cup: the bread and the cup of promise, the bread and the cup of remembrance, the bread and the cup of hope.

Life happens around the table, in the making of meals and

memories, in the sharing of food and friendship. And, on this night, it all came down to a meal for Jesus and those who loved him.

What is the bread and the cup of promise?

The bread and the cup of promise is Christ Jesus our Lord. We come to receive the promise of his life in ours.

I read the passage about Peter denying he even knew Jesus—not once, but three times, each one more vociferous. Then he heard the rooster and remembered he had broken his promise to be true to the end. Later, it was in a meal by the sea that the promise was restored because of who Jesus was in his life.

What is the bread and cup of remembrance?

The bread and cup of remembrance is Christ Jesus our Lord. We have come to remember Jesus and his life in ours.

The opposite of remember is dismember: to take apart. When we re-member Jesus in this meal, we put the Body of Christ back together again. The call to re-member we are one in the Spirit is a call to remember love is an act of will, not an emotion.

What is the bread and the cup of hope?

The bread and the cup of hope is Christ Jesus our Lord. We have come to renew our hope in him and his life in ours.

Jesus shared the bread and cup with his disciples and was dead by the middle of the next afternoon. They knew nothing of Easter. They only knew the one they had trusted had been executed among common criminals. They ran. They hid. They went fishing. They went to the tomb. When it comes to acting out the Easter story, we know the cross is not the Last Word, yet in our daily lives, we, like the disciples, have no idea what tomorrow holds. We know only the pain and promise we find in today, and the hope we have mustered and saved from days gone by, based on the love we have found to be true. Or, perhaps untrue. Hope is keeping on. We hope when we set the alarm clock for tomorrow morning, when we plan whatever's next, when we look beyond all that so easily besets us, when we sit down together for dinner.